Michael,

Thank you fc
sharing your inspiring
story with us.

Debi Comie

What people are saying about *Loving Failure*

A deeper-than-usual dive into business finance, Debi Corrie expertly covers the broad scope of business finance. I appreciate how she breaks down various business components in such a way that both experienced and new entrepreneurs will benefit from her insightful book.

Dr. Ivan Salaberrios
President and Owner
AIM Technical Consultants

Whether you are a new or seasoned CEO or CFO, this book is a refreshing, easy-to-read guide on your path to business success. If you are new to these roles, this book provides a reliable road map; if you are seasoned, it's a great refresher course on winning strategies. I love the detailed table of contents and this book will live on my desk as a quick "pick me up" reference guide for running a financially healthy business.

Dr. Mitra Ray
Author, International Speaker,
Entrepreneur and Wellness Advocate

Impactful! This book is a no-nonsense, common-sense approach to running your business. As an entrepreneur for over 30 years and a Business Mentor, I look for simple, solid approaches to help my clients run their businesses with efficiency. This is the "How To" book that my clients will all be receiving. Read this book!

Phil Black
Business Mentor

Debi nailed it! Debi understands the crucial need for cash flow in every business and offers this book as a guide for small business owners to understand the basics of a financially healthy business. She further explains the step-by-step process for how to create and sustain a healthy business model through the uses of good ole' relationships that many have thought were "outdated". This book is clear, concise, and devoted to assisting companies of any size navigate financial prosperity.

Colleen Biggs,
Chief Inspiration Officer,
Lead Up for Women

If you are senior executive in a large corporation or small business professional, the day you stop learning is the day you should start doing something else. Debi Corrie's book, "Loving Failure": Getting Control of Your Business Health", is full of constructive advice to help you learn from your mistakes, plan for your company's future, and make sure you have the financial stability and security your company needs to thrive in the future.

Well worth your time to enjoy the quick read from one of the industry's most knowledgeable professionals on financial wellbeing — especially in today's highly competitive business climate.

David Corson, Publisher/Editor
Commercial Construction & Renovation, Commercial
Kitchens, Federal Construction, Craft Brand & Marketing
Commercial Construction & Renovation Summit
Commercial Construction & Renovation People

LOVING FAILURE

Getting Control of Your Business Health

DEBI CORRIE

DJC Media, LLC

LOVING FAILURE
Getting Control of Your Business Health
Debi Corrie
DJC Media, LLC

Published by DJC Media, LLC, Maryville, IL
Copyright ©2020 Debi Corrie
All rights reserved.

Editor: Kay Uhles

Cover and Interior Design: Davis Creative, DavisCreative.com

Publisher's Cataloging-In-Publication Data
(Prepared by The Donohue Group, Inc.)
Names: Corrie, Debi, author.
Title: Loving failure : getting control of your business health / Debi Corrie.
Description: Maryville, IL : DJC Media, LLC, [2020] | Includes bibliographical references.
Identifiers: ISBN 9781735990309 (paperback) | ISBN 9781735990316 (ebook)
Subjects: LCSH: Business enterprises--Finance. | Profit. | Industrial management. | Business enterprises--Valuation. | Success in business. | BISAC: BUSINESS & ECONOMICS / Entrepreneurship. | BUSINESS & ECONOMICS / Finance / General. | BUSINESS & ECONOMICS / Strategic Planning.
Classification: LCC HG4026 .C67 2020 (print) | LCC HG4026 (ebook) | DDC 658.15--dc23

ATTENTION CORPORATIONS, UNIVERSITIES, COLLEGES AND PROFESSIONAL ORGANIZATIONS: Quantity discounts are available on bulk purchases of this book for educational, gift purposes, or as premiums for increasing magazine subscriptions or renewals. Special books or book excerpts can also be created to fit specific needs. For information, please contact DJC Media, LLC, debi@acumaxum.com.

Dedication

This book is dedicated to my grandfather. He inspired me to help business owners be successful in their businesses and personal lives. His story will always inspire me to help others achieve their goals and help them understand how to manage money in their businesses.

For my life partner, David: You allow me the grace to dream big. You believe that I can do anything I decide to do. This book would not have been possible without your support and love. You are always my devil's advocate to make sure I think things through.

To my mother, who taught me that the world is a hard place and so what. She inspired me to concentrate on what I have control over and not what I do not. From her I learned that obstacles are only roadblocks and I can find another path to my goals. She taught me that I am responsible for my journey, for my own successes and own my failures.

For my tax practice partner, Kristene Rosser Schmitt: You inspire me to be my best and live life to the fullest. It has been one of my greatest joys to be in business with you. There is no other person that I would rather do life with. I can't wait to see what we can accomplish together.

This book is also dedicated to business owners who want to build sustainable businesses and who want to understand how cash and numbers can be used to grow them. These business owners are the backbone of our economy. I admire your bravery, tenacity, and entrepreneurial spirit. I hope my message will help you with your own business success.

Table of Contents

Foreword

It's a sad truth that many great companies fail because of completely avoidable financial mistakes.

Knowing your numbers and how to make critical decisions around those numbers can be the difference between just making it and soaring in your company.

Running a business, no matter what level you are at, is not for the faint of heart. It takes hard work and commitment. It takes the willingness to leap even if your plan is not perfect. Also, it takes courage to fail which can be your biggest motivator toward growth. Although most of us know that's only part of the equation. You need the correct strategies, structures, and systems in place... otherwise you will end up running yourself into the ground, only to walk away at the end of the day with nothing to show for your big efforts.

Having mentored hundreds of CEOs from startups to global enterprises, I can tell you that this is true whether you have been in business for one year or 20 years. As someone who has been there personally (a few times), trust me when I say it is 100% worth your time to know your numbers and build a sound strategic plan around them.

I can also tell you that in uncertain times such as these, getting a grip on your finances can be the difference between your company flourishing or barely surviving.

That's where Debi Corrie comes in. Debi is a member of my business mentoring company, Pinnacle Global Network. When I discovered her ability to help businesses make smart strategic decisions with their numbers, I was beyond impressed, I knew she had a special gift and powerful insight around numbers that all business owners need.

This book answers each and every financial question you've had about business — along with the ones you haven't even thought to ask. It's the ultimate comprehensive guide to ensuring financial success (in your business and in your life). I have written two books on business and I've read hundreds of others. I cannot recommend this book, *Loving Failure*, highly enough.

There are few people who are as qualified to walk you through this journey as Debi is. If you follow her wisdom, you won't just create stability in your company, you'll finally be able to create the lasting, high-level growth you've been looking for in your business.

If you're a business owner, you have put your blood, sweat, and tears into your company, and now you deserve to turn that into a life of success and joy. It can be scary when you're in the dark about what to do next with your processes or money — yet *Loving Failure: Getting Control of Your Business Health* will shine a bright light for you and walk you through toward your big goals every step along the way.

Allison Maslan, CEO of Pinnacle Global Network
Author of *Scale or Fail: How to Build Your Dream Team,
Explode Your Growth, and Let Your Business Soar*

Introduction

This project has been a long time in the making. Originally, I had envisioned this book as an inspirational book about successful people. In fact, I had interviewed several successful entrepreneurs only to find out that success was based on the ability to fail. Successful people fail multiple times in their lives and businesses. It was these failures that taught them the most meaningful lessons in their lives and that would propel them to the next level in their businesses because they knew what had not worked and they could try other options.

What was interesting about this project is I learned that successful people do not dwell on their failures for long periods of time. They are single-minded in their quest to create successful businesses and desired outcomes. They do not take "No" for an answer. They are tenacious in their desire to make things happen and to move on to the next steps in business.

The things I thought would make people successful, such as chance and circumstance along the way, turned out not to be true. Luck had nothing to do with success. In many cases, it was years of hard work that turned the successful person into an "overnight success." People would never know the grind of their lives in the early years. There were lost nights of sleep along the way, employee difficulties, financial troubles, and cash issues. Would they make payroll? Could they pay their vendors? Could they pay themselves?

These business owners were concerned about their employees as much as they were about their own successes. They built cultures that nurtured people. They understood profit margins. They developed processes for business. They were not afraid to make decisions. They did not wait for perfection to make a move. Most of them did not start out this way. They learned these lessons over time.

As I am writing this book, the world is facing uncertainties with a global pandemic. This virus has not only affected us as a society; it has devasted businesses with poor cash flow. It has been a death sentence for businesses that were struggling before the virus hit. And it has also proven to be a driving force for people to find new avenues of success. It is not the struggle or the outcome that matters; it is how we handle what happens next that is important.

We may have had the foresight to have cash set aside. We may have been approved for a PPP (Paycheck Protection Program) loan or obtained other funding in this crisis. What is important is how we handle our cash during the pandemic and what we choose to do next. As business owners, we never know what is around the corner and trying to second guess could put us in decision purgatory. Indecision is our biggest enemy in a crisis.

Successful people look to the future, grab opportunities, and do not look back. Many business owners will not survive this crisis because they did not grasp the implications of not understanding their business numbers, financials, and cash flow. Cash is the key to any business's success.

 TIP: Think of ways to increase your cash flow now. What new project or idea have you been wanting to try? What other income stream can you create for your business? The time for innovation is now.

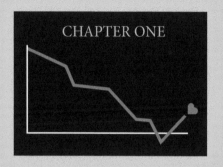

CHAPTER ONE

The Finance Decoder Ring

People ask me all the time why I started my business. It was because of my grandfather, who was born during the Great Depression. He knew hardship. As a young man, he served in the Navy and was deployed as a cook on a ship. He served in the big war, World War II. When he returned home, he apprenticed as a plumber. My grandfather was good at this work and decided to start his own business. As the business prospered, his sons worked for him. When his sons left the business for college, he hired a couple employees. He had built a successful business that provided for his family. He owned his shop, a cottage on the lake, and his house. He was not a rich man by any means, but he was comfortable.

At the age of sixty-two, my grandfather decided to retire. There were just a couple problems with his retirement:

- He had not set aside money for his future. He enjoyed life and had spent what he earned.
- He had not always filed a tax return. No one had ever explained to him that his social security benefits would be based on the income he reported.
- His retirement was going to be based on his social security checks; so, because he had not filed tax returns or claimed a profit, his social security checks were incredibly small.
- He thought he would die by age sixty-five. In that time, men retired from the factory or other jobs and

literally died a year or two later. Therefore, my grandfather thought he would live for a couple more years and then die. That was his retirement plan.

By the time my grandfather died at age eighty-two, he had lost everything he owned. Here was this big strong man who had worked his entire life and had nothing to show for it. He was a proud man. He became a ward of the state when he entered a nursing home because Medicaid would pay the costs. The family did not understand what financial trouble he was in until it was too late.

As business owners, we only know what we know. If we don't know the right questions to ask or have the right team surrounding us, we could end up like my grandfather. It is my goal to help business owners avoid ending up like him. Every business owner needs to know how to handle finances and needs to know the business options available.

When my grandfather retired at sixty-two, he did what many do: He closed his business by shutting it down and telling his customers to go somewhere else for their plumbing needs. That was the easy way to end his business. What he did not understand was that he had a lot of options.

- He could have continued to have two employees and continued to draw funds from the business.
- He could have decided to rent his shop and have drawn a monthly income.
- He could have had a succession plan for his business and buyout payments as part of his income for several years.
- He could have sold his customer list.

There were many creative ways that my grandfather could have continued to draw an income without working in his business. But he did not choose any of these options because he did not know he could do them. He did not have a good understanding of the money that would be necessary in his retirement.

The Importance of a Tax Return

My grandfather did not understand the importance of his tax return. As an entrepreneur and business owner, he wanted to hold on to his cash and not pay the IRS. He thought not paying taxes was the best option for his business. And we all know the consequences that resulted. My grandfather's strategy may not be the best for business or personal financial security.

The next worst thing for any business owner is filing a tax return which shows a loss every year. In fact, showing losses year after year may result in some devastating consequences.

 FAIL: Sole entrepreneurs who filed Schedule C tax returns in 2019 and showed a loss were unable to get PPP loans from their banks and created a cash failure. PPP loans were forgiven by the government if used to pay payroll, rent, and other business expenses during the 2020 global health crisis. The business owners who showed a loss in 2019 missed out on this free money.

Continual losses will adversely affect business and personal net worth. A business that continually shows losses will probably not be able to obtain a line of credit or get a conventional bank loan. And business credit may affect personal credit. Continual losses also will affect some business owners' ability to obtain a personal mortgage or other form of financing.

Financial statements and the financial condition of a business affect the ability to achieve goals. Typically, banks, buyers, and other financing institutions want to review business and personal tax returns before lending money. They want to make sure the business has worth and that the business owner is creditworthy. Tax returns and profitability of the business affect a bank's approval for financing and interest rates; they also have an influence on the worth of the business when the owner is ready to sell or transfer it.

 **TIP:** Ask yourself these questions:
What are the goals for my business?
Do I want to sell my business?
Do I want to pass it on to the next generation?
How does my business affect my personal finances?

If a tax accountant is telling a business owner to buy equipment to reduce taxes, they may not have that business owner's best financial business interest at heart. This is by no means their fault. A good tax CPA's number one priority is to save their clients taxes. This strategy, however, may not coincide with the desire to create a sustainable and self-sufficient business. Profitability and generating the cash needed to sustain and prosper are the keys to any business's success.

Major equipment purchases that are not necessary will use cash for purposes that do not align with business goals.

A tax accountant should be asking clients questions about their business. They should be able to provide information about tax deferral and tax-planning methods that reduce the tax burden and help keep their cash.

Just because a company is profitable does not mean that they have to pay the IRS any more than it is due. Depending on the industry and the business, there are tax strategies that a tax professional can help with to minimize the tax burden.

Tax returns are used for many things. A banker or an outside lending source will want to see a company's tax returns before they lend money to see if it is a good financial risk.

Debunking Banking Myths

A secret that most people do not understand about bankers is that they are risk-averse. It is a misconception for many business owners that they do not need to look for a loan from a banker until they need it. This is the wrong time to go to the bank and get a loan.

Myth # 1—Banks will lend me money when I need it.

When a business is having cash-flow problems, the bank does not want to lend them money. Bankers want to know that the loan will be paid back, so when there are cash-flow issues, it is hard to prove that the loan payments can be met.

One of the first things that I do for my clients is analyze their creditworthiness. Business credit, like personal credit, can be improved to be acceptable by the bank. It is critical that a business have a line of credit. A line of credit is a revolving account for short-term loans when cash is short. Operating lines of credit can be used for payroll, to buy inventory, or for other short-term loan needs for everyday business expenses.

Myth #2—I don't need a line of credit. My business does not need cash.

Think a business does not need a line of credit because cash is good? Go back a couple paragraphs and read about bankers again. Remember, bankers want to lend money when the company has cash. Sounds counterintuitive, right?

Recently, I onboarded a new business owner and analyzed their cash needs. This business had a small line of credit from the bank and had just picked up a major new client. The business owner's new client was going to require a large cash outlay for inventory. After looking at the business's cash flow, I told the business owner that we needed to request a larger line of credit from the bank. The business owner was afraid the bank would not approve the loan.

I accompanied the business owner to the bank. We took the most recent financial statements and the purchase orders from the new client. We sat down together with the banker and explained the new business opportunity. The bank approved the line-of-credit increase in about two weeks.

The business's new client received their first shipment. But there was a problem with the inventory, and the new client refused to pay the business owner until the issue was resolved. Eventually, the business owner resolved the issue and was paid within sixty days. The order was so big from the new client that the business owner would have had to cease operations without the increase in the business line of credit. Needless to say, the business owner was grateful we had increased the line of credit.

Myth #3—I am not bankable; my banker turned me down for a loan.

Not every bank wants to finance every type of loan. Some banks only want to do real estate or equipment transactions; some will finance the purchase or sale of a company; some will issue lines of credit, while others will not; some bankers will not like the industry served; others will like it and will approve a loan or line of credit. Businesses just need to know who likes their business model.

In my experiences, one of the lessons learned for many business owners during the 2020 pandemic was that the business relationship with their banker was critical to their business's success. Many companies had not had a relationship with a business banker and did not understand its importance.

Remember, bankers are there to help. A banker should be a partner in good times and in bad. A good banking relationship helps to grow the business and will help weather storms in a company. Bankers should understand the specific industry of their client and its common practices. It is important for business owners to develop the relationship, so when a tough conversation comes, they have an ally.

Internal Financial Statements

Accounting financial statements are a living, breathing documentation of business. These internal documents are just as important to a business as tax returns and bankers.

Most business owners are familiar with profit and loss statements, which shows if a business has been profitable or not profitable for the month. But there are two other key internal financial statements important to businesses: the balance sheet and the cash flow statement.

The balance sheet tends to be ignored because it is not understood. In fact, it is probably the most misunderstood report by business owners; however, without the balance sheet, there is no true picture of the business. I have dedicated Chapter Seven in this book to take the mystery out of the balance sheet and the impact it has on businesses.

The profit and loss statement records sales, costs to make products, and expenses for the business. Information about every company department is on the profit and loss statement, balance sheet, and cash flow statement. It is important that business owners understand how the processes and procedures of different departments affect profitability, which is possible to learn through these documents.

A long time ago, I met a business owner who thought the accounting department created reports that had nothing to do with the company's financial performance. I was literally floored by this philosophy. What I did not understand was that the financial statements were not being presented each month with the right information. At the end of the year, huge adjustments needed to be made to these reports which caused the business owner not to believe the numbers presented. Putting myself in that business owner's shoes, I would have believed the same thing.

Because she was not receiving the correct information each month, she could not use her numbers to help her assess the business. She could not use her financial statements to make sound business decisions. This caused her to believe that numbers were just some made-up figures that had nothing to do with her business.

TIP: It is critical that your monthly reports are correct. You should have a finance team to make sure that your books are properly closed each month. The skill of the people handling the data is an important component of receiving correct financial statements. They should print financial statements to be reviewed by you and your chief financial officer (CFO).

Financial statements are tools to help increase cash and profitability; they should be used to make decisions about a business. Financial reports show what the company is doing well and where there is room for improvement. They do not predict future performance, but report past performance. The business owner is in total control of the future and decisions made, and as such, should be aware of these reports and their uses.

Profits in a business are important. When I hear owners say they are not in business to make money, that does not make sense to me. Without profits and cash, a business cannot be sustainable.

According to the U.S. Bureau of Labor Statistics, "Approximately twenty percent of new businesses fail during the first two years of opening, forty-five percent during the first five years, and sixty-five percent during the first ten years. Only twenty-five percent of new businesses make it to fifteen years or more."[1]

TIP: Learning about your business's financial health helps to create a successful business. The number one reason businesses fail is because they do not have cash. Cash is the cornerstone of any business. How cash affects every aspect of your business is covered in Chapter Eight.

As a successful business owner, you should:

- Understand your market and the value you provide to customers. You should have a clear understanding of your product lines and how to leverage your message to reach your ideal market.
- Have a realistic business plan and share it with your employees. You should also have created timelines and goals to achieve your objectives.
- Be flexible and understand that technology has an impact on business and that the needs of your customers change over time.
- Have a marketing plan to generate leads for the business and track your progress and lead conversion.

---

1 "Survival of private sector establishments by opening year," (Rep. No. Table 7) (n.d.), https://www.bls.gov/bdm/us_age_naics_00_table7.txt

- Have a good relationship with your bank and maintain cash reserves to survive business ups and downs.
- Understand your financial reports and what drives profitability for your business.

As you read this list, think of the areas where you could use some assistance. Is there someone on your team that can help you? Is there an outside resource that you can use? Business strategies you can use to accomplish these goals and sleep at night will be discussed in Chapter Nine.

Successful business owners know that numbers and people go together. Behind every number is a person— employee or contractor—and that person can make or break a business. Employees want to work for the business and want to help it succeed.

Chapter Six is devoted to how to help employees understand key numbers that produce financial results without having open-book management.

When we are born, we are fearless. Our parents teach us about fear to protect us from danger. They teach us our first limits on what we can do with that fateful word "No." This became clear to me when my son was two. I said "No" to him one time too often, and he got upset with me. He performed what I call the "No-No" dance. He literally shook his finger and fist at me to get his point across, as he danced across the room telling me, "No, no, no." I still laugh about this memory today, but it made me take a different tactic with him.

As we mature, we are programmed to be careful, successful, and risk-averse. Not to fail. But as entrepreneurs, we must be risk-takers to be successful. Decisions are about taking actions in our businesses without knowing the outcomes. Each decision has one of two outcomes: success or failure. Either way, we have a decision to make before the next move. Indecision prevents movement in any direction at all and will eventually result in failure. We must be willing to fail (take risks) to move the business forward.

It has been my experience that owners who are indecisive create the biggest risks for themselves. Like the gear shift in a car, if it is stuck in neutral, the car is going nowhere fast—or at all. It is the same for businesses in a state of indecision. Inaction keeps the business from moving forward. Maybe it is the fear of adding the first employee because leadership is unsure of how to cover the cost. Maybe the business wants to offer a new service, but managers do not know how it will be received. Maybe the company does not want to look at financial numbers because they are afraid of the results.

We each have decisions to make. Are we willing to take our car out of neutral and learn how company numbers can make us more successful? Are we willing to look at where we are today and start making the changes necessary to have a financially successful and healthy business in the future?

There are ways to analyze financial risk on big decisions and initiatives without being a mathematician or a finance whiz. As business owners, we need to understand the risk of our decisions. With good number analysis, the financial impact of decisions on our businesses can be analyzed. This does not mean the decision will be successful. In fact, the most successful people we know have made bad business decisions. Knowing the financial consequences of an unsuccessful outcome versus a successful outcome can help when making financial-risk decisions.

People who are successful fail all the time. In fact, our brains are not programmed for success. We learn our best lessons from our failures. Ask any successful business owner who has obtained "overnight success." They will tell us about the ten years of hard work, failure, and grit it took to get there.

As I conclude Chapter One—"The Finance Decoder Ring," I will continue sharing stories about companies I helped and the lessons we learned together while analyzing risk and what it takes to make a successful business. Each chapter to follow addresses important questions for business owners to know:

Chapter Two—"The Teeter-Totter of Sales and Cash"

Everything in business starts with sales processes and the sales team. This knowledge will help business owners answer the following questions:

- How can we hold people accountable for their sales progress?
- What metrics can we use to hold sales teams accountable?
- How does the sales pipeline help predict future cash flows?

Chapter Three—"The Price Is Right—How to Create Value"

Let's look at the elements of pricing business services and products. Below are questions to help a business owner create value:

- How does pricing strategy affect cash flow?
- Do discounts help or hurt business?
- How can a company increase prices for goods and services?

Chapter Four—"Where did all the margin go?"

Understanding margins and why they are important in business is vital. Margins determine how much cash a business can generate. Business leaders would benefit from knowing the answers to the following questions:

- How is gross margin for a business determined?
- What is a profit margin?
- How do margins affect profitability?

Chapter Five—"Data, data—Who's got the data?"

Businesses are bombarded all the time with data and statistics, which are important parts of any business. Knowing the answers to the following questions is critical:

- In the world of big data, who should handle the management of data?
- Who are the players on a financial team and what are their responsibilities?
- How can data and statistics be used to run a business?

Chapter Six—"Score big: Give Employees The Rules To Win."

The days of employees blindly following instructions are over. I say thank goodness that millennials, who make up much of the workforce today, want to understand what business values are and what the business's big picture is. Business owners should be able to answer the following questions:

- How do employees engage with management?
- How much financial information should be shared with employees?
- How can the answer to these questions dramatically improve a company's bottom line?

Millennials have changed the way we see business and are the future of our workforce. Through them, businesses can learn new technology and how it can save time. Millennials are generally in tune with this type of work culture which can increase business profits.

Chapter Seven—"The Black Hole Called the 'Balance Sheet'"

As I said earlier, the balance sheet is one of the most misunderstood reports and is rarely looked at by business owners. But the balance sheet holds some key information that every business owner needs to understand. Without the balance sheet, there is no complete picture of their company. Business owners should be able to answer the following questions:

- What assets does my business have?

- What are my financial obligations?
- What are financial ratios and why are they important?

Chapter Eight—"Predict Cash Flow"

It is possible to predict future cash flow. Like any part of business, cash flow takes planning. Business owners should learn the answers to these questions:

- How much future cash is available to the business?
- What tools can be used to estimate the business's cash needs?
- What investments make sense for the company?

Business owners do not have to be the ones to complete the cash flow report, but they do need to understand how to spend money wisely within the business. Chapter Eight covers tools that will help in conquering this skill.

Chapter Nine—"Business Owners Should Be Planners, Not Dust in the Wind"

A business plan is something that is critical to financial success. Companies that do not plan do not reach their goals. Business leaders will find answering the following questions to be helpful:

- What are the future goals for the company?
- Where do I want the company to be in three to five years?
- What is a strategic plan?

There is a difference between having a dream and executing a plan. A useable strategic plan can be developed.

Strategy is not static; it is innovative and progressive toward a business's goals.

Chapter Ten—"Myth Busters: Understand the Monthly Facts"

Most business owners have a good sense about sales in their businesses. They need to understand other aspects of the business as well, such as:

- What information should be reviewed on a weekly basis?
- How should the team put together a monthly financial package?
- How does past information improve future performance?

TIP: Learn how forecasting can provide real-time information to guide your financial results.

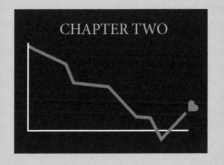

CHAPTER TWO

The Teeter-Totter of Sales and Cash

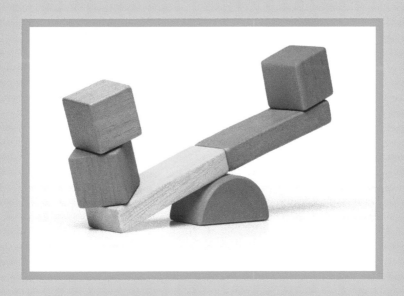

Every business starts with the sale. Without sales, businesses cannot generate cash. When looking at cash flow, owners need to understand their sales cycle, their dollars in the sales pipeline, their target market, their sales team, and their sales goals. Understanding how these four things interact will help to determine how to generate the sales needed to be successful.

The Sales Cycle

"Sales cycle" is the time it takes to convert a lead into a sale. This time will vary depending on the services or products sold, and it is dependent on whether products are bid or purchased outright.

A company's sales cycle determines how quickly they will receive cash to cover business expenses. Many software programs can track this information.

TIP: You may have heard of HubSpot, Sales Force, Less Annoying CRM, or Pipedrive. All of these software packages will track leads, closes, and sales dollars. Like any software they only work if they are used. Figure out the main drivers in your business and what you should track. Different software packages will work better for different industries.

Dollars in the sales pipeline

If a business works strictly on proposals, the dollars in the sales pipeline are the life blood of the business. The sales pipeline will track where the next cash opportunities will be found. For companies that have long closing cycles, tracking this information allows the company to know if there is a hole is the cash pipeline and if there will be an interruption in the cash flow of the company. It allows the sales manager, accounting team, and CEO to know where business is coming from and when.

One of the most powerful statistics to track with proposal work is the probability of award. Proposals with a low probability of award should not be worked on by the sales team. The sales manager should determine if low probability work should be bid. This allow the sales manager to analyze the viability of the work being brought in by the sales team.

For one of my clients the probability of award helped them redistribute the amount of work to be bid and get more project awards. The sales team concentrated on projects that were winnable and their closing rates increased.

When I structure the sales pipeline report for companies, it includes the following information:

- Date the proposal was received
- Customer name
- Type of revenue stream
- Amount of the proposal
- Proposal due date
- Probability of award

- Amount of revenue to be generated based on the probability of the award
- Proposal awardee

This information has many implications for businesses. It can be used as a great way to streamline processes, determine competition, look at the closing rates of sales personnel, and point out route areas of improvement in sales processes.

TIP: The sales pipeline report identifies companies that consistently use you as that second or third proposal and will never award you work. It can quickly identify proposals that the team should not be spending a lot of time on. Most of the time, I recommend that any proposal that has the probability of award equal to or less than fifty percent be passed up by the sales team. If you do not believe you can get the work, why would you spend the time on the proposal? Spend your time on your money-makers, not on proposals that are high risk and low margin. This report clearly outlines where your future cash flows are likely to come from. It allows you to have discussions with your sales manager and sales team about the actions that need to happen so the company can make their sales goals.

The first time I utilized the pipeline system was in 2001 after 9/11. I was the controller of a small engineering firm that did capital projects for big players like General Electric, Harley Davidson, and other OEM (original equipment manufacturers) companies. For six months following 9/11, we heard nothing from our major competitors or customers. When working on capital projects like this, lead time could be six months to a year before the project comes to fruition, but after 9/11, businesses were unsure what direction to take. Capital projects for us came to a standstill. We started using this pipeline report to track our outstanding business and the probability of award. This report became a critical part of our weekly meeting, showing projects outstanding and future cash available to navigate the company cash crunch left by six months of silence from customers. The pipeline report helped the company president focus on the jobs that could be awarded and spend valuable time on the right things so we could win deals. This idea worked so well that I have continued to use it with my customers today.

Using technology for sales and engaging sales teams are important to overall business success. There are two types of salespeople: hunters and gatherers. Depending on the size of the business and how customers are attracted, both are needed to be successful.

The sales team

Hunters are salespeople that get their own leads and close deals for the company. They work best on base salaries and are interested in their commission plans. They want to be rewarded for the deals that they bring to the company.

Gatherers have leads come to them. They focus on customer service and maintaining current customers. They do not seek new business on their own; new leads may come from marketing campaigns, phone calls, customer referrals, and other efforts not initiated by the gatherer. Think of gatherers as your customer service team.

FAIL: Cash failure often results from hiring the wrong type of team member to increase sales and the customer base. Gatherers will maintain customers; hunters will increase sales and cash flow. Both are important members of the team.

Whether team members are hunters or gatherers, business leaders need to know the metrics for a successful sales team. Many companies have targeted sales goals each year but have no idea of how to make these goals a reality.

TIP: Share your sales goals with your sales team. Each month have a targeted sales amount for each salesperson, account manager, or customer service representative on your team. These goals can be based on the prior year's metrics. For example, say you had sales of $10,000,000 last year and you want to increase sales by ten percent or $1,000,000, for a new sales goal of $11,000,000. You would need to give each salesperson their goal for the year and month to meet this metric. These goals need to be perceived as attainable by the sales team. If team does not believe the goals are attainable, they will not be met. How do you give yourself a reality check? Work backwards from your sales goal.

To work backwards from the sales goals, business leaders have to know a couple of metrics: First, what is their average sales dollar amount? Based on that number, then they can calculate how many sales they need to add to hit the company sales goal.

Say the average sale is $1,000. One thousand more sales for the year would be needed to hit the new company goal of $11,000,000. Let's break that down even further. That is eighty-three additional sales a month (1,000 sales per year / 12 months) or nineteen new sales per week (1,000 sales per year / 52 weeks).

Sales target for the year: $11,000,000
Increase in sales year over last year $1,000,000
Average sale: $1,000
Amount of new sales needed: 1,000
New sales per month: 83
New sales per week: 19

Now that we have some numbers, we can look at the reasonableness of the goal split between the team members responsible for the sales. With the information above, we have good intel to know if the team has the bandwidth to accomplish this goal or if we need another hunter or gatherer to handle the influx of sales.

In my prior life in the transportation industry, we calculated our customer retention rate in order to project the number of buses needed to attain our yearly sales goal. Our contracts renewed every two to three years, so we had to know our probable retention number and the amount of new business that was needed to reach our sales goal.

Using the formula above, businesses are able to set sales goals and know the amount of sales necessary to obtain them.

But how do these businesses keep their sales team accountable for their goals?

Sales is a numbers game. Businesses need to know the number of qualified leads it takes to win a proposal or approach a prospect before the sale is made. Whatever that number is needs to be met by each salesperson each week. Each salesperson needs to track their number of contacts, hot leads, and sale closes. They should also be tracking the dollar amounts associated with each of these activities.

Correctly tracking contacts is imperative to sales staff reaching their goals. "Contact" means a conversation with a person. Sending emails, texting, and leaving phone messages do not count as a contact; there must be a reply and engagement from the person contacted. Likewise, reaching out to a customer twenty times to clarify needs or send material does not count as an additional contact. Each contact should be gauged by the sales process the client is in. When a new stage is reached, the next conversation is counted as a contact. Getting clarity on the contact number will help the sales manager have a productive conversation with each sales team member.

Once the number of contacts per salesperson is determined, that number needs to be met by each salesperson each week. Each salesperson needs to track the number of contacts, hot leads, and sale closes. They should also be tracking the dollar amounts associated with each of these activities.

TIP: If you have never gone through this process, you are most likely going to get pushback from your sales team. They will tell you that they do not have time to track this information. But this data is important to understand your sales lead time, the number of qualified leads, and closing rate. You need to know these numbers for the company as a whole and for each sales team member. The process must be monitored and encouraged for the team to complete. It is part of their weekly accountability meeting with the sales manager. Make this information visible to all sales team members.

If your sales team is hitting their sales goals, a weekly meeting with the sales manager is not necessary; however, if they are not hitting their sales numbers, then coaching and a meeting with their sales manager is absolutely necessary to review their numbers and progress and to, perhaps, get some friendly competition going. Make it part of their commission sales plan to turn in this information. It is a great way for the sales manager to have a productive conversation with the sales team and to track how well each salesperson is doing. You, as the business owner, need to find out where the gaps are to help your sales team be successful.

What if the sales team is not selling the discontinued products or company specials that need to be cleared? Managers need to make sure that the sales team is aware of all company specials and what the incentives are to sell discontinued product. Employees want to know what is in it for them. Good salespeople understand their commission structure and will sell items that get them the most commission.

TIP: If the items you want to sell or programs you want to promote are not working, take a look at your commission structure. Your commission structure should be set up to drive the results that you want from your sales team. Remember when we were talking about hunters earlier? They want to know how they will be paid on deals. Hunters will work toward their goals based on their commission program.

Sales Metrics to Understand

Let's look at some critical numbers to understand sales and the impact these numbers have on cash flow.

Number of sales per month

The number of sales per month is just like it sounds. It is the number of actual sales per month compared to the target number for the sales team. This tells the business owner if the company is on track to meet their sales goals for the month and the year. When the sales team falls behind on the company sales forecast, the sales manager needs to determined which months will be increased to get the sales team back on track for the sales goal.

The number of sales per month tells the sales manager the productivity of the sales team. It shows the amount of deals that must close to meet the monthly sales goal number, which varies depending on what is sold.

Why is the number of sales per month important? Take a car dealership that sells Ford Fusions versus a car dealership that sells Jaguars. Each dealership sells to a different audience and has different gross margin percentages. The Ford Fusion dealership has to sell twice as many cars to make the same top-line sales amount as the Jaguar dealership.

How many Ford dealerships are there versus Jaguar dealerships? Audience and price point make a difference in how much the business needs to sell.

Average sales dollars per sale

When calculating how to get to a sales goal for the year, the average sales dollars per sale can be used to determine the number of sales needed to reach the future goal. The calculation is:

Total sales / Number of sales = Average sales dollars per sale

For example, if we had $5,000,000 in sales and the number of sales was 50,000, we would have an average sales dollars per sale of $100.

$5,000,000 sales / 50,000 sales = $100 per sale

If we set our sales goal for the coming year at a ten percent increase over last year's sales of $5,000,000, our new sales target is $5,500,000. To reach that goal, we would need to have 55,000 total sales:

$5,500,000 sales / $100 per sale = 55,000 sales

What if we decided, instead, to increase the dollar amount per each customer sale to $110? Now you can sell to the same number of customers.

$5,500,000 in sales / $110 per sale = 50,000 sales

TIP: Here is the power of a price increase. If your average sale is $100 and you institute an annual price increase of four percent, your average sales price automatically increases to $104 per sale. That means you only have to upsell an additional $6 on each sale.

I hope you can see how powerful this information is when determining how to structure your sales goal for the coming year. It can help leverage your current customer base to increase your sales power. More sales equals more cash.

Think about the last time you were on the Internet looking at purchasing an item. Did the company website make other suggestions as well? Most companies have software that automatically helps them get additional sales with suggestions to purchase items together. This software is like having your sales team visit customers 24/7. How can you use technology to increase your sales to your customers?

Customer retention rate

The customer retention rate is the number of customers a business holds on to every year and who buy again and again. The customer retention rate helps determine how many new sales and new customers are needed every year to hit the sales target. The higher the retention rate the fewer new customers and sales that need to be acquired for the period. It always costs more time and money to acquire new customers than it does to retain a current customer. Knowing the retention rate is one of the key drivers to reaching sales goals. To calculate it:

(# of customers at end of period - # of new customers acquired)
# of customers at the start of the period

Multiply this number by 100 to get the percentage. For example:

- # of customers at the beginning of the period 100
- # of customers acquired   20
- # of customers lost   10
- # of customers at the end of the period   110

Now we can calculate customer retention:

110 customers at end – 20 new customers = 90
90 / customers at the start of the period 100 = .90
.90 x 100 = 90% retention

Tracking customer retention can be tricky, especially if working in a seasonal or one-and-done industry. The ability to get repeat customers is critical to increasing the worth and the cash flow of a company.

The number of apps and software that can be used today to track this information and have reports generated without using an Excel spreadsheet is amazing. The software and packages can be evaluated based on business size and goals. I find this information critical in industry segments that do a lot of proposals, such as legal firms, accounting firms, construction industries, and architecture firms.

TIP: If you are not in the above industries, you may be wondering what you should be tracking for your sales. If you are on an e-commerce platform, you should be able to track this data electronically through their reporting system. For example, you should know the amount of abandoned carts (in other words, when customers did not purchase your product) so you can analyze why people are not buying your products. You should be able to easily see the average amount of sales with your e-commerce software.

With an e-commerce platform, you automatically generate your customer list as they purchase products. The platform keeps track of what customers have purchased, how often they purchase, and the products they like. All the information is there. It's up to you to utilize it to better optimize your sales. There are many ways to track information and accumulate data, methods which will be discussed later the book.

What if you are in an industry that has one-off sales, such as construction or repairs? Find a way to work with other businesses on some type of joint venture arrangement so you both can benefit from sales. Negotiated business gets you out of the low-price game.

One of the easiest ways to increase customer retention rate is for businesses to provide a monthly service, maintenance agreement, service agreement, or contract. Finding a way to generate monthly recurring revenue in the industry can create better and more dependable cash flow. For example, the below innovative companies have figured out how to retain repeat customers:

Dollar Shave Club provides a monthly subscription for razor blades. The company was founded in 2011 by Michael Dublin. The premise was simple: Sell a monthly subscription for razor blades for about a dollar per blade per month. Dublin used video to promote the company and put the market on notice. The company sold for one billion dollars to Unilever in 2015. Dollar Shave Club remains a separate company and now sells wipes, shaving gel, and other products.

Chewey.com is an online pet e-commerce site that sells pet food, pet products, and pet over-the-counter medicines. It has created a monthly auto-ship club for its members to make purchases effortless.

 TIP: If you have an e-commerce site, what can you do to sell a monthly kit or service to your members or customers? Can you have the customer pick their monthly products? What creative ways can you make your cash flow better with monthly repeatable services?

Think outside the box to generate other forms of revenue for cash flow. If you are a professional-services provider, is there a monthly subscription or program you can create surrounding your services? Don't think about what you cannot do; concentrate on what you can do.

Below are examples of entrepreneurs that pivoted and innovated during the 2020 global health crisis.

A dance school in San Diego, California, was declared a non-essential business and was shut down during the pandemic. The business owner had traditionally held classes in her studio and could no longer do this. She looked at her business and figured out how to offer dance lessons online to students that were no longer coming to school. Her business, which would have generated no revenue during quarantine, now provides a revenue stream. Before, in the brick-and-mortar location, she was limited to her region; now, she teaches dance classes all around the country. And she set it all up in less than ninety days.

Katie's Pizza and Pasta was a restaurant that catered to dine-in customers. During the pandemic, the owner, Katie, added online frozen pizzas to the business. Katie began to flash freeze pizzas and started selling the new frozen pies online. This whole process happened in just ninety days. She now sells her pizzas all over the country, in addition to selling them at her two eateries.

My point is that only business owners put limits on the ability to sell. Only they can limit the possibilities of their revenue streams.

Let's talk about marketing and its impact on sales. The first thing to understand is that marketing and sales are not the same thing. Marketing is what helps the company get leads and builds their brand and reputation. The sales department brings leads into the business and closes on those leads.

Marketing is a critical function of sales. The marketing team and the sales team must be aligned to have a successful company. The branding and sales messages must be the same. In today's world, people check out businesses on the

Internet; they know about the business and its leadership before they reach out to them. The business's digital presence, the website, and the employees represent that company.

TIP: Your website is your company's introduction. It should be mobile-friendly, easy to navigate, and provide key points about you and your business. If you sell products on your website, it should be easy for customers to navigate, make purchases, and pay.

Whether you like it or not, your company's relevance will be judged by its website, through which potential customers or clients will evaluate your business, your brand, and digital technology. In today's world, prospective customers will already have formed an opinion based on your digital footprint. Make sure you are putting your best foot forward.

Customer acquisition cost (CAC)

Customer acquisition cost, or CAC, is the measure of total sales and marketing efforts per the number of new customers acquired. Sales and marketing expenses include salaries of sales and marketing personnel, apps and software, tools, such as websites, brochures, and other marketing materials. To calculate:

Total cost of sales and marketing / # of new customers

Customer acquisition cost will tell how long it takes to recoup the cost of acquiring a customer and making a profit. Tracking this metric can help hone in on sales strategy and make improvements in marketing and sales campaigns to gain more customers and drive down costs.

Lifetime Value (LTV)

Customer lifetime value calculates the amount of future profit and future cash flow a customer will generate. It helps to focus on the lifetime relationship of a customer rather than short-term profits. The length of the customer relationship is called the "customer lifespan." To calculate LTV:

(Average purchase value × gross margin × purchase frequency × customer lifespan) – CAC

The goal is to get the LTV to be greater than the CAC cost for the customer and have the customer turn a profit for the company.

Website Statistics

If a business is an online shop, it should be using software that tracks customers and their activities. Many e-commerce software packages help track this information. At a minimum the company should be tracking:

Visitors indicates the number of people that visit the website, not the number of times they visit. Each person is counted in the time period.

Referrals are sources that generated the traffic to the site. This could be social media sites, a customer referral program, or lead magnets.

Bounce rate is the number of people that visit your site and click the back button. This could indicate that they found a wrong site or that they didn't see what they wanted on the page. Reducing this rate is critical to customer conversion.

Exit pages denotes when people leave the page. We expect people to exit pages, like the order-processed page. Analyzing which pages are exited and why they are exited can help to create better customer engagement and conversion.

Lead Conversion Rate is the number of visitors that completed the goal. It may be a lead magnet and registering their email; it may be completing a contract or a sale.

Top-Ten Pages shows what pages customers visit the most and feel are the most important? The knowledge of top-ten pages informs the business owner what visitors find the most engaging. By knowing this information, business leaders can drive content to engage more visitors.

Marketing

It is important that companies, in their business planning, put some money aside for marketing. This money is not just for the website but for everything related to the business; that is, printed material, catalogs, books, software, or other company offerings.

Marketing is hard to measure; it has many intangibles that are qualitative rather than quantitative. The first intangible is building brand recognition. How can a business determine what their return on investment is? The return on investment is the ability to get new sales and have name recognition. Name recognition and branding can determine the value of the product and the price to charge. We will be going through this in detail in the next chapter when we talk about pricing.

Branding and digital marketing are not the same thing. Digital marketing can be measured by a return on investment, or ROI. Unlike branding that is subject to opinion, digital marketing is measured by the number of qualified leads it generates. These qualified leads are then turned into sales for the company.

When hiring a digital marketing company, business owners should be asking questions like:

- How many leads can I expect for the month?
- How will I be using lead magnets?
- How many site hits can I expect?
- Will the digital marketing company help me create lead magnets?
- Will weekly reports from the digital marketing company be shared?
- How will we determine when things need to be recalibrated?
- Will the digital marketing company give examples of clients who worked within the specific industry and will they share the results?

The same questions can be used to hire a digital marketer for the company. Marketing results are very trackable and business owners should always be able to measure the results they receive. The important thing is to make adjustments to drive the correct results.

As we see businesses change their models in the midst of the 2020 pandemic, it is important to remember that the world is constantly changing. Although this is an historical event for the world, it will not be the last time we experience something of this magnitude.

It is important that we, as business owners, keep abreast of things going on in our industries, to be aware of new technologies, to see how we can use them to improve sales and business position. Businesses that are not growing are dying. That doesn't mean that we have to have a business that grows exponentially. We do, however, need to be aware of what's happening in the world around us and see how we can utilize this new information to improve services to employees and clients.

As new technologies becomes available to track sales, business leaders should reach out to prospects and find new ways to digitally engage people; they should look to the team and outside resources to help.

CHAPTER THREE

The Price is Right –
How to Create Value

Imagine a company is having one of the best sales months ever and then finds out that it lost money for the month. How is this possible? What is happening with the financial statements?

One of the most impactful things a business can do is not only pivot and try new things, but also price their business services and products correctly.

Businesses make money via pricing. Pricing determines what business sector to sell in. Let's take a cup of coffee. We can buy coffee at McDonald's for a dollar $1 or a cup at Starbucks for about $2; we can buy a McDonald's latte for $2.79 versus Starbucks for $4.79.

These are obviously two different pricing models and they each sell something different. McDonald's is a fast-food model for cheap food; Starbucks sells an atmosphere on an upper scale where one can hang out, use Wi-Fi, and work or study. They both are successful businesses that appeal to different customers. Each makes a different gross margin and pays its employees differently.

Brand perception and quality are perceived by the price point that is set and the perceived value of the product. Look at the difference between a Honda Civic and a Ferrari. A lot more Honda Civics have to be sold to make the same margin that Ferrari makes. It is like comparing the products at Walmart to the products at Saks Fifth Avenue. They are at a different price point and margin.

FAIL: Business owners who promote their business as the lowest price to clients in their market create a cash failure. Low price is a losing proposition for a privately held businesses.

Companies like Walmart, Amazon, GE, or Home Depot can get better product costs from their wholesalers because they leverage their economies of scale. These mega businesses can buy in volumes that a smaller, privately held business cannot typically get close to. This allows the mega merchandisers, like Walmart, to sell at a much lower price point. If a company is trying to compete in this market, they are fighting a losing battle. In fact, they are probably not making a profit.

 **TIP:** The time to take a look at your pricing strategy is now. Why now? Because if your price is not right, your business will not make a profit. If your business does not make a profit, you will not have positive cash flow. If you do not have cash in the bank, your business will have a tough time recovering from the current global health crisis or any crisis in your business.

This will not be the first or the last time that we, as a nation, will face economic challenges. Successful business owners understand that some cash must be left in the business to survive economic downturns and to have assets for bank lines of credit. They must have cash to make infrastructure investments, such as software, tech, marketing and advertising, employee hires, et cetera.

TIP: Are you ready to meet the challenge next time there is an economic downturn? As you are reading this chapter, you may think that it is impossible to compete with anyone except by price. This simply is not true. There is a secret sauce to your business. You need to figure out what differentiates you from your competition.

Before we take a deeper dive into the price discussion, you have to know some important numbers about your business. This will help you determine if you have set the right price for your products or services.

The Business Breakeven Point

So how does a business know if their price is correct? It all starts with the business breakeven point. Business owners need to know their business breakeven point to determine how much they must sell to make a profit.

FAIL: The business not knowing how much cash the company needs to cover the operating expenses and loan obligations for the business is a cash failure.

The business breakeven point calculates the amount of sales needed to cover all business expenses. When the breakeven profit for a business is calculated, the profit number is zero. Zero is the starting point of any business. Companies must know how much they need to sell to cover annual business costs. Annual business costs include the costs to make the product or services, wages, and other monthly business costs, such as rent and utilities.

The breakeven point of every business is different. It is not even the same for all competitors in a given industry. Breakeven points will be higher when the business must cover high fixed costs and low-margin-producing products. For example, if a business has high operating costs, such as expensive rent, high variable costs, and excessive payroll costs, it would result in a higher breakeven point for the business.

TIP: A word of caution to new business owners. If you are just starting out and making this calculation, it would be a mistake to assume that your staff will remain the same size as you grow the business. Take a look at what your business would look like if you were operating with a full staff at your target business goal. To set a price with only you as an employee will set yourself up for failure. You will never be able to cover the higher fixed costs that will be incurred as you grow. Make sure you are looking at what your business will need for employees and overhead in three to five years. We are trying to calculate your breakeven point, not your go-broke point.

For a legacy business or a business that has been around for five to six years, the breakeven point is much easier to calculate. Historical data will help when working the calculation.

Figure 1 includes a worksheet which provides a framework to help calculate a business's breakeven point. Variable and fixed costs are needed to calculate this number. A financial professional can help calculate this number with more accuracy and detail.

Once a breakeven point is found, a business owner can determine many things; for example, the amount of sales needed every year to cover expenses. It can quickly point out if the business must cover high fixed costs or product costs to make a profit. Every sale after the breakeven point contributes to the profitability of the business. It is literally money in the bank.

To calculate the business breakeven point, you must know your variable and fixed costs.

Variable costs

Variable costs are directly correlated with producing product or service. For every sales dollar produced, there is a direct correlation to the cost per dollar.

In Figure 1, a service industry that makes the majority of its profit on labor costs, the variable costs are high at sixty-four cents for every dollar of sales. It sells some products, but at a small markup.

Figure 1

Breakeven Sales Target	$1.093,772	
Variable Costs		**Variable Costs %**
Cost of Goods Sold	$ 200,000	18.3%
Direct Labor	500,000	45.7%
	700,000	64.0%
Fixed Costs		
App Expense	$ 5,000	
Wages Office	200,000	
Systems Admin Expense	15,000	
Sales Expense	5,000	
Banking Expenses	5,700	
Marketing Expenses	2,000	
Insurance	1,500	
Cleaning	6,000	
Lease Expense	36,000	
Interest Expense	10,000	
Security	1,500	
Telephone & Internet	12,000	
Miscellaneous	1,000	
Medical Insurance	5,000	
Professional Fees	40,000	
Depreciation	20,000	
Office Supplies	12,000	
Postage and Delivery	1,000	
Software Subscriptions	12,000	
Employee Relations	3.072	
Total Fixed Costs	$ 393,772	
Total Costs	$1,093,772	

Below are different scenarios to calculate direct labor costs. Remember, business owners only need to understand the components. The company CFO will do the actual calculation.

For a manufacturing company, their variable costs might include:

- Direct labor to make the product, including wages, payroll taxes, and employee benefits
- Materials needed to create the product
- Inbound freight, import fees, and duties to bring the materials to the manufacturing plant

For a distribution company, the variable costs might be:

- Purchased product
- Inbound freight, import fees, and duties to bring the product to the business

For a service industry, the variable costs might be:

- Direct labor to complete the service, including wages, payroll taxes, and employee benefits
- Purchased product used for the service
- Inbound freight, import fees, and duties to bring the product to the business

The bigger the company the more complicated this section of the profit and loss statement can look. Finance teams handle the details.

Fixed expenses

Company overhead expenses are fixed expenses needed to run the business. These expenses include rent, advertising, internet, telephone, utilities, and so on. The most common fixed expenses are:

- Warehouse expenses
- Advertising
- Banking fees
- Commissions
- Salaries and wages
- Payroll taxes
- Employee benefits
- Commercial insurance
- Dues and subscriptions
- Apps and software
- Repairs and maintenance
- Rent
- Leased equipment
- Travel
- Professional services
- Memberships
- Tax and licenses
- Office expenses
- Trade shows
- Marketing
- Depreciation
- Telephone
- Temporary labor
- Utilities
- Bad debt
- Miscellaneous expenses

These expenses are fixed; they must be covered and considered when calculating sales price and the amount of sales necessary to break even. As companies scale, overhead tends to increase and more manpower is needed to handle different functions.

In Figure 1, for every dollar of sales over $1,093,772, thirty-six cents goes to the bottom line. If the company increased sales $100,000, it would generate $36,000 more in cash. This exercise can be eye-opening for a business that is struggling with cash flow or having trouble making a profit.

A business produces cash and profits based on the price set for products and services. If the price is too low, the cash and profits needed to be successful will never be produced. The right amount of cash and profits will allow a company to meet their obligations and have a sustainable business.

 TIP: Setting a price for your products is not just about cost and profit; it is about your mindset regarding price, value, and money. It is your mindset about your value, the value of your employees, and the value you bring to your clients. Typically, when a new business starts, the owner prices themselves too low because they are afraid to ask for the price they deserve. This mindset is rooted in your philosophy about money.

 FAIL: Businesses allowing negative perceptions about cash and money to affect the price they set for goods and services is a cash failure.

Our perceptions of money and the ability to believe in our own products and services greatly affect our pricing. Many of us were taught that money and the rich are unscrupulous.

That is simply not true. Money is not the root of all evil. Money provides opportunities to people to make life decisions. It gives people financial freedom.

When business owners make money, they can help more people in their community, church, or the world if they choose. They can reward their employees for meeting financial goals or give them pay raises.

Let me assure you that making money and a profit is a necessity in business. It is not a luxury or something to be ashamed of. It is okay to support your causes and your employees. It is okay to draw a salary from your business. It is okay to be successful.

Remember, one of the reasons you went into business for yourself was to control your own destiny. Money allows you the opportunity to accomplish your business and professional goals. Be proud that you have created a successful business.

What Comes Next?

Once a business owner knows their breakeven point, they can then take this information and determine price. They need to be able to answer the following questions:

- How many products or services do we need to sell to break even?
- Has the company achieved this number before?
- How many customers do we need to sell to?
- Can we hit the number this year based on our sales cycle?

- What corrective actions do we need to make with our sales team to hit this goal?
- Do we need to change our marketing to align with this new goal?
- Does this sales goal make sense?

The calculation of the products or services needed to reach the breakeven sale number:

Total sales for breakeven / The average sales order size =
The # of sales necessary to reach the breakeven point.

I realize this calculation is simplistic when, in actuality, it can be a complicated process for multiple product lines and services. Figure 1 is for purposes of building a framework around the breakeven point. The company's strategic CFO should be able to help dive into the details of this calculation and help to answer the following questions:

- Has the company ever sold the number of products or services required to break even?
- Do we have enough manpower and/or inventory to accomplish this goal?
- Does the sales amount seem plausible?

If the answer is no to these questions, it may be time for a strategic price increase.

 FAIL: It is a cash failure to not increase the price for the company business goods and services on an annual basis.

Initiating an annual price increase with customers should be part of an annual planning strategy. Customers are not going to ask for an annual price increase. It is the business owner's responsibility to determine the amount of the increase and initiate the conversation. What I can say for certain is that the company's vendors are increasing their prices, employee benefits, insurance costs, salaries and so forth. Look at big stores and big companies. They are doing one of two things: negotiating lower prices to get better margins with their vendors or they are instituting price increases on products. Or both. Typically, price increases are so small that they are not noticed.

Consider new car prices. Every year, manufacturers create new makes, models, and other items to increase their prices on vehicles and trucks. They may offer sales to move their merchandise, but they are counting on people wanting to get the newest car, early. These consumers will pay close to list price to be the first to own the new vehicle model.

The easiest way to lower the breakeven point is to raise price. Many companies that hire me do not increase price annually, but it is one of the first things we talk about in a strategy session because it is the best way to bring money to the bottom line immediately.

Concerns About Raising Prices

Business owners may have concerns about raising price. Below are some of the most common.

I will lose customers

Concerns over losing customers typically occurs when a company has to do a major price adjustment to cover all those years a price increase was not initiated. It is highly unlikely that customers who like a company's products or services will leave after receiving a three- to four-percent price increase a year, as long as that business is still delivering value.

When a business needs to institute a major price increase, say fifteen to twenty percent, then a customer may leave. I do not recommend this pricing strategy unless the company has some major commerce events that can justify this type of price increase. Below are some situations where it may be necessary and acceptable to do a major price increase.

Example #1. An IT service provider provides a yearly price to customers for IT-managed services. Suppose the customer price was not correctly calculated because the customer needed more of the IT provider's time due to equipment issues and unforeseen events. At renewal time, it would be appropriate to review these issues with the client and explain that a price increase is necessary for the IT service provider to maintain the business. Would the client leave?

I recently had a client in this situation. They were able to retain their customer and get the twenty-percent increase needed on their contract. They had a well-thought-out strategy and were able to share facts with the patron to justify the price increase. The customer was very satisfied with the service and was willing to accept the price increase based on the information my client had shared.

The above scenario was a win-win because each party received a benefit: My client made a profit on his customer after losing money on them for over a year; my client's customer got a fair price and great service.

Example #2. The transportation industry is an example where the commodities may have an impact on price; that is, the price of oil has a direct impact on the price of fuel. In the transportation industry, fuel can be one of the biggest costs for a business. It is common practice to implement a fuel surcharge in times when fuel prices are high. If the company does not add a surcharge and their competitors do, they are leaving money on the table. The customer is not going to ask for a price increase, but they will understand a temporary fuel surcharge for high fuel prices.

Example #3. A company imports products and is affected by an unexpected tariff imposed on the goods. This happened in 2019 in several industries, including steel. Prices paid to import steel skyrocketed, causing a ripple effect through the steel industry. It was necessary for many steel businesses to increase their prices to cover the cost.

It does not make sense to sell products at a loss to maintain pricing with a client. The bottom line cannot afford to absorb the cost.

Competition is not raising their prices

Business leadership should worry less about what the competition is doing and make sure the customer understands and appreciates the products' and services' value, and how they benefit them. When a price increase is necessary, the customer should receive an explanation about why the price increase has been initiated. Maybe the business invested in logistics software that will allow the customer to receive products sooner; maybe a major supplier initiated a five-percent price increase that the business must now pass on to its customers. Company personnel should explain where the money is going. In instances where the business has a small price increase of two to three percent, it might not be noticed by the customer and no explanation is needed.

The business has always run on low price

Maintaining historical low pricing has never been, nor will ever be a good pricing strategy. It is time to get out of the low-price game. Low price is not a sustainable business strategy. There will always be someone else that can offer a lower price. Small businesses cannot compete with Walmart or Amazon. This strategy does not make good business sense and will result in companies receiving lower profits and less cash.

TIP: Have you ever watched two gas stations in a pricing war? This is especially entertaining when the gas stations are located across the street from each other. Eventually, one gas station has to stop lowering their price. No one wins.

A much better strategy is to concentrate on your unique selling proposition, or "USP." Your USP is about defining what is unique about you and your company. Simon Sinek presents a Ted Talk called "How Great Leaders Inspire Action," in which he talks about the "golden circle," shown on the next page.

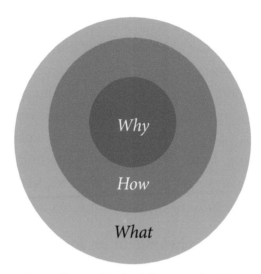

Communicate from the inside out; that is, start with your "why," not your what or how. Your why will sell your product. Your why creates an emotional connection to your customer. Brain science is behind this, saying that people do not buy what you do, but why you do it. Check out Simon Sinek's talk.[2]

I recommend to clients that they examine how their business is different from the competitor's business. This knowledge helps clarify the differentiation in order to explain it clearly to prospective customers. I suggest exploring the answers to the below questions:

- What is my competitor's why?
- What types of clients do they like to work with?
- What do they offer that no one else does?
- Do they cut product to order?
- Do they sell in unusual quantities?
- Do they take returns, no questions asked?

2 Simon Sinek, "How great leaders inspire action," TEDxPuget Sound (September 2009), https://www.ted.com/talks/simon_sinek_how _great_leaders_inspire_action

- Do they provide return labels for their products?
- Do their offer a monthly subscription with valuable content?
- Do their have a free giveaway?

These are all unique selling propositions. Small businesses are profitable when they do not compete with big-box stores and when they sell their why and value, not their price.

Understanding these concepts can reframe the mindset about value provided to clients and justify pricing structure. The entire team should understand the business's why and the value that it brings to customers. This mindset helps marketing campaigns be successful; it helps the sales team be successful; it builds the confidence needed to sell products and the company's value.

The Difference between Retailers and Wholesalers

Selling product to retailers, wholesalers, or distributors is a different business model than selling products online. Retail price will only be paid by consumers. Wholesalers typically want to purchase product at fifty percent of whatever the retail price is. Selling to wholesalers or distributors can be a great strategy, as long as the product is priced right. When considering going from a retail market to a wholesale distributor market to increase sales, business leaders need to understand both retail and wholesale concepts.

Wholesalers and distributors must make a profit on product like retailers must make a profit on goods. The television show *Shark Tank* often addresses the cost to make the product. If product costs can be kept at twenty-five percent or less, the business will make a profit in both wholesale and retail markets. How much profit is made will depend on the type of product sold, too. This topic will be covered more in Chapter Four when we talk about gross market margin and profitability.

Pricing Strategies: The Secret Sauce

When a company has multiple products, it is important for them to develop a pricing strategy. Managers should look at their products and determine the best sellers. It is easier to raise the price on best sellers because people want these products and will normally not balk at the price.

Some businesses increased their prices during the 2020 pandemic. For example, meat prices rose due to plant closures; restaurants added surcharges. The global crisis created a great time to get the price right.

For slow-moving items, it is probably not the best idea to raise the price. Instead of a price increase, companies may want to consider lowering prices to move the inventory before it becomes obsolete. But lowering prices can be hard for business owners to do, especially if they feel they will be losing money. The fact is, though, they have already paid for the inventory; they have invested cash to purchase the inventory. It is always better to have cash on hand rather than the product collecting dust on the warehouse shelf.

One of my clients is a distributor and used this idea to sell their slow-moving products. They created a bundle special for the customer that included one of their best sellers and one of their slow-moving products. They have been successfully using this strategy to turn slow-moving items into cash.

TIP: Consider offering a BOGO (buy one get one free) or maybe pricing a slow-moving product at a discount when purchased with a best seller. The idea is to create a package that can help get the slow-moving product out the door. Remember, customers also love the word "free." Depending on what you sell, your product may be donatable to a charity. One of my client business owners had a business yard sale and then donated the leftover product to charity. The client was able to take the cost of the product as a tax deduction. This allowed them to clear their shelves of obsolete items that could be put to good use by another organization.

Do not let fear keep you from doing the things that will make your business profitable. Imagine what a well-thought-out price strategy could do for your business. Be creative. What could you do with the cash that you get from selling the inventory collecting dust on your shelves?

CHAPTER FOUR

Where Did All the Margin Go?

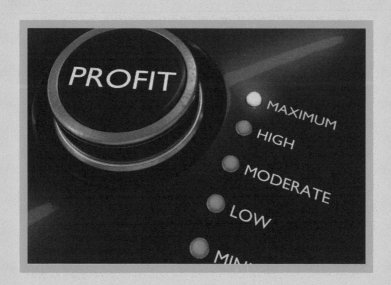

A question I often ask clients is, "When you are looking at your profit and loss statement, do you go to the last page first?" We all have a tendency to do that. We want to get to the end of the story first. However, if we skip the events leading up to our profit number, we are missing a big part of the story. Imagine starting a movie and fast forwarding to the end before deciding if we want to watch it. Knowing the ending spoils the story. The same thing is true of a profit and loss statement. The profit and loss statement tells the story of a business for the month, quarter, and year.

Sales for the Company

When we do not read the report and go to the end first, we are missing all the juicy details of the plot. First of all, we miss knowing how much of our sales dollars we kept. Business accountants should set up reports to include, at a minimum, total sales for the month, sales discounts, and sales returns. These three numbers host a wealth of information.

Figure 2

ABC Company		
Profit and Loss Statement for May 20XX		
Gross Sales	$500,000	
Sales Discounts	(2,000)	0.5%
Sales Returns	(10,000)	0.2%
Net Sales	$487,500	

Gross sales are all sales before sales discounts, customer returns, and merchandising fees. Businesses should report gross sales before merchandising fees from services like Amazon, eBay, Etsy, credit-card processors, and other payment venues. This allows the costs for these types of services to be analyzed and seen on the company books.

In Figure 2, we have discounts of five-tenths percent for the month and a two-percent return rate for merchandise. These two numbers are important to track. They can help a business owner decide how to handle product returns and analyze if discounting makes sense.

Let's take the car industry for example. Dealerships have a list price for the car and then typically negotiate the sales price. The list price of the car is the gross-sales price. The difference between the negotiated price and the gross-sales price is the discount. TIP: Does your discounting programs make good business sense? In studies of discounting programs in relationship to price, you will most likely find that discounts do not drive your sales; your sales team does. Discounting is an easy way to close the deal, but may not be in the best interests of your product or brand.

Evaluate the amount of business that you are discounting and determine the gross margin for the product. Are you making money or giving away the farm? The improper use of discounting and sales can also devalue high-end products. Customers will get used to sales and only make purchases when the product is discounted.

If you are a retail store, this may be part of your marketing strategy to bring in customers. Kohl's, a national retailer, uses this pricing strategy to bring customers into its stores. Make sure your gross-sales amount for the product is priced high enough to leave you with a profit when utilizing discounts.

Cost of Goods Sold

Second to sales, the most important information for a business owner to understand on a statement is the cost of goods sold or the cost to make product or provide services. For companies that manufacture products, their cost of goods sold includes the labor and the materials to make the product. For a distributor or wholesaler, this would be the purchase price of their products, plus any freight or import costs to bring the materials or product to the plant or warehouse.

Figure 3

ABC Company	
Profit and Loss Statement for May 20XX	
Cost of Goods Sold	
Product Costs	$100,000
Direct Labor	
Wages	110,000
Payroll Taxes	11,000
Benefits	22,0000
Total Direct Labor	143,000
Supplies and Tools	1,200
Total Cost of Goods Sold	$244,200

In Figure 3, product costs, which are the costs to buy or make merchandise, are $100,000. Direct labor costs are the costs of employees or subcontractors to create the product, produce the product, or install the product. For ABC Company, the direct labor costs are $143,000. Supplies and tools are items that are not inventoried but are used up in the production process. ABC Company spent $1,200 for tools and supplies.

Gross Margin

The difference between net sales and cost of goods sold is called "gross margin." Gross margin is the profit from sales that will be used to pay salaries, marketing, and other administrative expenses. In Figure 4, the net sales for ABC Company is $487,500 and the cost of goods sold is $244,200, for a gross-profit margin of $243,300. This money will be used to pay the rest of the business expenses, such as employee salaries not related to production, advertising, marketing, rent, and so forth.

Figure 4

ABC Company	
Profit and Loss Statement for May 20XX	
Net Sales	$487,500
Cost of Goods Sold	244,200
Gross Margin	$243,300
Gross Margin %	49.9%

There are basically two levers to increase gross-margin percentage: sales price and cost of goods sold. We have spent a lot of time talking about the impact of sales price increases. In the next example, Figure5, the company has increased their price by three percent. This results in $300,000 in additional sales. The impact of the price increase also increases the company gross margin by 1.4 percent (55.6 percent - 54.3 percent). Imagine what could be done with an extra $300,000.

Figure 5

ABC Company
Profit and Loss Statement for May 20XX

		3% Price Increase
Net Sales	$10,000,000	$10,300,000
Cost of Goods Sold		
Product Costs	2,500,000	2,500,000
Direct Labor		
Wages	1,500,000	1,500,000
Payroll Taxes	150,000	150,000
Benefits	300,000	300,000
Total Direct Labor	$ 1,950,000	$ 1,950,000
Supplies and Tools	120,000	120,000
Total Cost of Goods Sold	$ 4,570,000	$ 4,570,000
Gross Margin	$ 5,430,000	$ 5,730,000
Gross Margin %	54.3%	55.6%
Gross Margin $ Increase		300,000

THEORY INTO PRACTICE

TIP: By now you may need to take a deep breath. Remember, you do not have to understand the details. Just the concepts. The most important part of this chapter is how you can get better gross-margin results. A financial professional can make sure that this calculation is recorded correctly for you and can walk you through the items that are pertinent to your business.

Understanding your gross margin and discounting programs is critical to increasing your business's profits.

How to improve the gross margin

One the quickest ways to add value to the bottom line is to improve the gross margin. For every dollar that we can save on our cost of goods sold, that dollar drops directly to the bottom line. Improving gross margin raises the profitability of the business and improves cash flow. It frees up cash in the business to be used for other business expenses, such as software, websites, production equipment, and other company assets. Below are strategies to improve the gross margin.

 FAIL: Having a low gross margin percentage compared to business competitors is a cash failure. The lower the percentage, the lower the amount of cash that will be available to cover other business expenses. The company gross margin should be equal to or better than the competition.

Reduce the costs of making product

Reducing the costs of making product can be done by negotiating pricing with suppliers. A question I pose to my clients is, "When is the last time that you sat down with your suppliers and renegotiated your price?" Like many of us, suppliers do not want to rock the boat. Many of my clients are surprised to learn, though, that when they push back on their supplier's price, they will receive discounts. This is especially true if the supplier has had a long-term relationship with the company.

Business owners should be aware of the following concepts, which may result in better pricing from suppliers:

- Does the supplier offer a cash discount for early payment? Many suppliers will offer cash discounts, from one or two percent, for payment terms of net ten or fifteen days.
- Is there a fixed price? When I worked in the transportation industry, we locked in the price for fuel from our supplier for an entire year in times of high fuel prices. This practice could save company money.
- Does the company offer an annual rebate based on purchasing volume? When I worked in the door-and-hardware industry, manufacturers offered rebates based on the number of doors and amount of hardware purchased. We were able to take advantage of the discount when we purchased the quantity required by the manufacturer for the year.
- Does the industry have a buying group membership? In the hospitality industry, belonging to buying groups meant better pricing.
- Is the company receiving the best deal and services? Comparative prices should be checked to keep suppliers honest.

A client in the steel industry told me once it was not possible to negotiate a lower price. I asked, "What could a phone call to another vendor possibly hurt?" The other vendor was very interested in my client's business and was willing to negotiate a price below that of the original vendor. By reaching out, my client was able to save costs and increase gross margin.

Turn over inventory faster

Inventory turnover is the amount of inventory that a business sells in a year. The more inventory on the shelf, the lower the inventory turn rate. Specific inventory turn rates apply to specific industries. A financial professional should know this number and help to determine the company's optimal turn rate.

TIP: Think of your inventory turn rate this way: With the amount of sales you have, how many times a year are you ordering stock or producing product for sale? The inventory turn rate tells if you are ordering too much stock and not having enough sales.

This is important for a couple of reasons. If you are purchasing large quantities of inventory that you do not have sales orders or customer purchase orders for, then that is cash that cannot be used for other expenses in your business. You could use that cash to pay for salaries, marketing, rent, or other fixed business expenses.

The costs of your overhead expenses for sales, advertising, and administrative expenses tend to be fixed for the month. When you turn your inventory faster, you lower these costs on a per-inventory-item basis.

Here is an example: Say it costs $50 to make your product and you sell 1,000 products per month:

$$\$50 \ x \ 1,000 = \$50,000$$

Overhead costs are fixed at $20,000 per month. Total costs for the month:

Overhead costs $20,000 / 1,000 = $20 per unit

Let's say, for the month, 1,200 products sold. Overhead per item drops:

Overhead costs $20,000 / 1,200 = $16.67 per unit

The more products sold the better the overhead rate the faster inventory will turn over and the more profits that are made.

For growing companies, this can become a stress factor; i.e., inventory is turning so fast that cash is constantly being used to buy more inventory. This is where a line of credit from the bank is essential to expand the business and meet temporary cash shortages. A business's relationship with their bank will help increase their line of credit to meet these temporary short-term cash needs.

One of the things I help clients do is get lines of credit. Having a financial professional on the team that has good banking relationships can help to find the funds needed to run the business.

Adjust the sales mix

I advise my clients to analyze which of their products are top-sellers and which are slow-sellers. With this knowledge, they can make sure they have plenty of top-selling stock and high-margin products; they can also align the sales team with the sale of these products.

For products that are slow-moving or have little profit margin, business owners should consider discontinuing them, eliminating the products permanently from their product line. Slow-moving products create obsolete inventory and lower gross margin. This may upset some customers, unless the company focuses on the new products they can provide.

Profitable businesses with good cash flow understand that they cannot please every customer every time. It is difficult sometimes for a company to tell a customer they will no longer carry a desired item. That is why a new product mix and new products are important.

Mary Kay had this process figured out when I was a sales consultant for them. Every quarter, they promoted a new line of cosmetics, labeled "limited editions," just for that three-month season. When the product was sold out, it was no longer available. The company kept an eye on their staple products, sprinkled in some new skin-care products, and eliminated low-selling items. Mary Kay has been consistent in this process, which works for them as a marketing plan for new items and gives their salespeople something to talk about each quarter to customers.

TIP: When you think about your products, ask yourself which ones should stay and which ones should go?

Automate your processes

Automation may allow a business to reduce payroll, produce a more consistent product, and increase inventory output.

For a manufacturer, their production line is the key to being efficient in the costs to produce the product. Several systems exist that can help employees involved in production to improve their processes. "Lean" manufacturing, derived from Toyota's 1930 model *The Toyota Way*, is used in many companies and is successful when implemented by employees, rather than by management.

If a manufacturing process is labor intensive, business owners should consider documenting the process so it is completed the same way every time. Repetitive processes allow employees to complete tasks more efficiently. Highly labor-intensive processes, like distribution, should be analyzed to make sure factories and warehouses organize products in the most efficient manner.

Documentation does not have to be written. I recommend that facilities—especially those with unique processes—use video, via YouTube or another platform, to record how the process works so employees learn by watching.

Analyze your customers

Business owners should be aware of their customer base and the customers that make money for them. Perhaps the success of this work can be replicated. Customers with high margins may be receptive to offers of up-sales by the sales team.

TIP: We all have low-margin customers and customers that use more of our time than the money received seems to justify. Consider systematically replacing low-margin customers with new higher-margin customers.

Consider spending more time with your high-margin customers. They are contributing positively to your cash flow; it does not make sense to provide more service to customers that are at a lower margin point. Freeing yourself from these time vampires will help you have time available for better customers.

Keeping the right customers is key to keeping your sales goals and margins. Focus on what customers you work with best and who align with your company philosophies. These customers will understand your value and your why and help you increase your cash flow.

Negotiate logistics and warehousing costs

Warehouse and logistics costs are major costs for distributors and manufacturers. It is important that company leadership understands the costs to ship products and ensures that the product price recoups these expenses.

Pricing from freight carriers should be reviewed and negotiated for set rates. UPS, FedEx, DHL, and other carriers will negotiate rates based on shipping volume and monthly use. Even the United States Postal Service has negotiated rates; however, services like PirateShip offer lower shipping costs than the main post office. All of these companies provide software to create labels and set up package pickups.

There are also several software programs that will automatically compare freight companies and the best shipping rates for products, rather than staff having to call each individual carrier.

 FAIL: Companies not reducing warehousing costs by eliminating or reducing obsolete and slow-moving inventory causes cash failure. This inventory is taking up space that could be used for better-selling inventory. If a distribution center is used, eliminating obsolete inventory will also lower carrying costs.

 TIP: Amazon is an inventory master. As product is purchased, Amazon makes sure that it is moving from their warehouses. Amazon charges a carrying fee for product that does not move off the shelves in a certain time period. Since Amazon's share of the product is based on sales, they want to make sure that anything stored in their warehouses is selling. Avoiding the warehouse fee is incentive for their shop owners to only stock product that is moving.

One of the first things I help business owners decipher is what products are profitable and what strategies can we used to improve gross margin.

One of my distributor clients had too many SKUs (stock-keeping units). When we looked at their product lines, some products had not moved in two years. We came up with a plan to move slow inventory, but concentrated more on expanding the products that were high margin. This resulted in the client increasing their gross margin five percent in the first year after implementing the plan. The extra cash was invested in software that produced data the company needed to make business decisions.

Net Profit Margin

After gross margin, there is another margin to track, that is, net profit margin. Net profit margin is the percent of profit made for the year based on sales before income taxes. This is the net cash that the company has left over at the end of the month to pay other expenses, like business loans and owners' dividends.

Improving net profit margin is all about controlling overhead expenses and making sure that money is spent in the right places for the business. A great place to start is for business owners to compare how they do business with how their competitors do business.

FAIL: When times are good, businesses tend not to pay much attention to overhead expenses; this is a cash failure. When times are bad, it is the first place they go to cut expenses. Think of the money that could be saved and the better profits earned for a company if they reviewed these expenses at least annually. Why waste money that could be used in some other area to expand the business and increase profits.

 **TIP:** Review your overhead expenses at least annually with your team and/or department managers. This review process will help assess your company expenditures.

Below are questions for business owners to ask to make sure that they are getting the best bang for their buck:

Advertising

Is the company reviewing programs and making sure that they still coincide with the results needed to grow sales or build branding? The CEO or marketing director should talk with a public relations firm to keep abreast of industry changes and practices.

Banking fees

Is the company bank competitive with other banks in town? Are they providing the value and services needed to run the business? Do they have mobile banking and remote deposit?

Commissions

Is the commission plan geared to get the sales results needed from the team? Does it need to be revamped to focus on the goals to be accomplished?

Salaries and wages

How are the top performers rewarded? Are the managers, supervisors, team leads, and employee team members the right mix for the company?

Payroll taxes

Are there any special tax incentives that the company can take advantage of at state and local levels?

Employee benefits

Do the benefit programs attract and retain employees? Are they affordable? Are there creative ways to offer benefits without additional costs to the company?

Commercial insurance

Does the business use a broker for commercial insurance? Do the coverages make sense based on the size of business? Does the insurance policy include cyber security? business shutdown insurance? property of others? employee fraud?

Apps and software

Is the company fully utilizing the apps and software that have been purchased? Do programs need to be canceled or upgraded?

Professional services

Are service providers delivering the value they promised? Does leadership need to revisit the business goals desired?

Repairs and maintenance

Is the business spending too much to repair and maintain equipment? If so, is it time to purchase newer equipment?

Leased equipment

Based on the cash flow of the company, does it make sense to lease rather than buy equipment? Who owns the equipment at the end of the lease? Who is responsible for equipment maintenance?

Travel

When is the last time the company travel policy was revisited? What types of company expenses will be reimbursed to employees? Are there caps on expenses for reasonableness?

Memberships

How does organization membership benefit the company or employees? What will be the return on this investment? employee goodwill? lead generation? sales?

Licenses

Does the company have all the licenses necessary to properly operate the business? Are there any certifications that could help increase sales and branding?

Office expenses

Does the amount of supplies ordered make sense? Are the items in this category actually fixed assets? Does there need to be a centralized ordering system?

Trade shows

What are the expected sales results for trade shows? Will the net sales from trade shows exceed the cost of the show? How much manpower will be needed? Will it interfere with the current sales effort? What is the expected return on investment (ROI)?

Marketing

How many leads did the program generate? What was the sales team conversion rate? How can the program be improved?

Utilities

How can the company save on utilities? Have they updated lighting? Do they practice energy conservation? Is there a cell phone policy? Does the telecommunication system need to be evaluated?

Temporary labor

Is temporary labor repeatedly needed to complete the workforce? Is a better process needed to reduce labor costs? Can better software be a solution?

Bad debt

Do company collection procedures work to collect past-due accounts? Is the credit-application process working correctly? Are the right clients on credit terms?

Answering these questions, which are geared to investigate and find better solutions, can open discussions about how to improve company performance. Business owners do not have to be the person with all the answers. If the team cannot help answer these questions, it may be time to look at hiring employees with more skills. As the business grows, it can exceed the skills of the employees on the team. To scale, the company may need to hire more experienced managers or C-suite executives. Hiring outsourced resources is a way to increase bandwidth without the cost of a full-time employee.

The above list of questions is not meant to be all-inclusive, but to get readers thinking about their own business expenses and how they can improve or utilize resources wisely to increase profits and sales. The mission is to make sure the business has the cash it needs to grow and creates cash reserves for times when business performance may temporarily be poor.

I am not suggesting that business owners be miserly. No one wins in that situation. I am suggesting that they know how they are spending money and making sure it aligns with the company goals and objectives. It is easy to lose sight of these expenses with a growing business.

CHAPTER FIVE

Data, Data—
Who's Got the Data

Today, everyone talks about data, and there are many software options and programs to calculate data. Where does one even begin and how can it help with cash flow for a company?

Some people believe that they will be replaced by data, but this is not true. The purpose of data analysis is to assist business owners in learning what drives sales and profits in their business.

Accounting records have important data that needs to be captured appropriately to reflect business performance. Accounting is a specialized industry and businesses need someone on the team to help. This could be an employee or an outside resource. It is important that the leader of a business focus on the tasks that can earn the most profits. Successful business owners surround themselves with experts that can help them achieve the success they desire.

The Numbers People

Every business owner needs qualified people to monitor data and make sure that it ends up in the correct buckets on their financial reports. Sometimes there is confusion about accounting positions and how they help us analyze data.

TIP: How do you start with this process? What if you do not even get monthly financial statements? What is the first step? Stop doing your books. Based on where you are in your business, you may want to hire a professional to help with your books.

If you are a solo practitioner, this is even more important. Outside resources can be hired to help with administrative tasks and bookkeeping. Think of the payback if
you are concentrated on the tasks that make money. You
cannot increase your income if you are doing tasks that do
not make money for you. You had the courage to start your
business, now have the courage to start your revenue-producing team.

Businesses that earn seven digits in annual income
should have at least an accountant on their team. When sales
are high, it is time to have an expert on the team to help
control data and issue financial statements on an accrual
basis.

This topic will be covered in more detail later. For now,
below are definitions and job functions for various numbers
people that may be needed on your team.

Accounting specialist process invoicing to customers,
accounts payable, and labor hours. They can pay vendor
invoices, run charge-card payments, and other transactions.
Typically, they are great at completing assigned tasks but
need assistance solving problems that are outside of the nor-
mal-day accounting tasks.

Bookkeepers enter transactions for the company. They
may do monthly journal entries and bank reconciliations,
as well as make sure accounting transactions are put in the
correct account buckets. They typically do not have an accounting degree.

Accountants typically hold accounting degrees and analyze accounting transactions. They make sure that transactions show up on correct accounting reports; they verify data and prepare tax returns and financial reports.

Controllers typically lead the accounting team and oversee the preparation of financial results. They deal with the company's historical data and help the company set up reporting structures, such as cost centers and departments, to analyze costs and overhead expenses.

Chief financial officer (CFO) is a senior executive responsible for managing the financial actions of the company. CFOs help to predict cash flow, execute financial planning, and analyze company strengths and weaknesses. They propose and implement corrective actions to improve company results. CFOs help the company change course and take corrective actions to improve financial results. Every company needs a CFO. That is why I formed my company.

Tax accountants should have a Certified Public Accountant (CPA), accounting degree, and understand tax strategy. A good CPA will review tax returns, recommend tax saving strategies, and provide quarterly tax payment amounts to the business's leaders.

CPAs and accounting firms are outside firms that can issue annual financial statements for a company. Banks, financial institutions, and bonding companies require the services of an accounting firm to issue financial statement reviews and compilations for outside parties. CPAs are licensed by the state and must pass a national test to provide these accredited services to businesses.

Accounting specialists, bookkeepers, accountants, and controllers report on the past of the company. They are the keepers of the historical data.

 FAIL: Inaccurate financial statements and/or no financial statements is a cash failure. Not understanding the financial position of the company can result in bad financial decisions that can hurt the cash position of the company.

The size of a company, the amount of information that has been accumulated, and the volume of transactions dictate who is needed on the team. Who is hired to handle historical data is essential to receiving the correct information each month for company financial results.

Many firms offer outsourced services. A business owner can do their own books, but is that where their valuable time should be spent? The business leader is the business-growth expert for the company. An outsourced CFO helps grow the business and can help analyze the strengths and weaknesses of the team; they can also provide training and best practices so that the finance team can deliver the right financial data.

Payroll professionals are outside service providers who perform payroll processes. The quickest way to get a business owner and their company into trouble is for them to do their own payroll. This is because the company must file and pay payroll taxes for their employees. Laws for payroll taxes are complicated. Leaders should hire a payroll company and have a specialist available to help. A payroll professional will make sure that all the reporting and deposit requirements for federal, state, and local taxes are followed. More importantly, the payroll service should be able to advise on any tax breaks that a company can get on taxes.

 FAIL: Carrying unpaid payroll taxes, likewise, is a way to get the owner and business in trouble with cash flow.

Payroll services are not expensive and can save time and money in the long run. Many payroll companies allow employees to print paycheck stubs, submit wage verifications, and check balances on vacation and paid time off. Business owners should stop spending time on non-CEO activities.

Cash Basis Versus Accrual Basis

There are two ways to report financial results: cash basis or accrual basis. Each method has its advantages and disadvantages. What method is best used to report the finances of a business?

Cash Basis

Although this method is very easy to use, it is not recommended for reporting financial statements. "Cash basis" means recording revenue when payment is received and recording expenses when invoices are paid. This method is acceptable for tax-reporting purposes but can play havoc on a business's profit and loss statements and balance sheets. Using this method typically results in a profit and loss statement that is positive one month and negative the next; it is also a method that makes it difficult for a business to determine its profitability. The recommended method for your internal reports is the accrual method.

Accrual Method

The accrual method records revenues when they are earned and expenses when they are incurred. This method allows business owners to determine if they are profitable by matching revenue and expenses in the same periods. The accrual method shows the true health of the business and helps to smooth company profits over time.

Software and Apps

Companies cannot scale without building a team. But they also cannot scale without investing in technology for the team. I see scaling companies miss the cash return on software and apps that can help their employees analyze data to improve cash and company profits for their business.

I know by now that your head is hurting just thinking about all the statistics that we have talked about. Besides software to manage these areas of the business, good data-keepers need to be on the team. Data-keepers are the people that are able to interpret and explain numbers to the CEO, if needed.

It is the CEO's job to be working on the business, not learning and running the numbers of the business. The CEO's mission is to build a good team to help interpret the numbers. The CFO will help the business owner decide what needs to be improved to get the results desired.

Investments in software need to be looked at like any major capital purchase. A company leader needs to think of a software purchase like hiring another employee on the team. The right software can increase the ability of a team to produce quality work and spend more time on the tasks that produce money for the company.

Software is an investment; it can track many aspects of a business. Software can organize the production team and warehouses to increase efficiency; it can also help make purchasing decisions based on what items are flying off the shelves and what items are outdated. Software should not be looked at as an unnecessary cost.

 FAIL: Investing in new software and not spending the money to properly implement the software and train the team is a cash failure. I have seen many companies miss opportunities to get the full benefits of new software because they do not understand all of its features.

Before purchasing software, a business owner needs to gather department heads and explore everyone's needs and expectations. They should evaluate the data that will be most useful to the company to achieve company goals.

Most businesses start with QuickBooks, Xero, Quicken, FreshBooks, or similar packages. These packages promise to make accounting simple and to collect data about a company and how it works. They are great packages to start a business but do not work well for companies once they reach about $5,000,000 in sales.

These programs are not equipped to supply the metrics we have been talking about needed to scale a business. Good software will be interconnected to each department's needs. It should easily integrate with other software packages to help track what is needed to run the specific company.

TIP: The first thing you, the business owner, need to decide is what data do you need to be tracking? Every business owner should know, at minimum, the company's statistics on return on investment (ROI) and financial ratios. Software to track these numbers will yield a high return on investment.

How do you know if you have the right software? If you cannot easily get this data from your software system, it is probably time for a software upgrade.

Below is an explanation of these metrics and why they are important to your cash flow.

Return on Investment (ROI)

Understanding return on investment can be used in a variety of circumstances. Most commonly, a business owner will use this metric to measure the return on investments for production purchases, such as heavy machinery, controls, software, or automation. It is used to determine if cash spent helped generate more company profits. The calculation of this investment is:

(Gain on the investment – The cost of the investment) /
(The cost of the investment x 100) = ROI%

This metric can be used on a wide variety of applications, for example, to evaluate whether the purchase of a company will be a good investment. ROI can also be used to evaluate real estate transactions and can be used to measure the return on marketing efforts.

Here's another example of how to calculate ROI for a marketing campaign. A marketing company is paid $10,000 to increase a company's sales. At the end of six months the marketing company has increased sales $15,000. The ROI would be calculated:

($15,000 sales - $10,000 cost) / $10,000 = 50% ROI

Knowing the results of a marketing campaign helps a business owner analyze whether it was a good investment for the company. Marketing campaigns are not built in one month and typically take several months for a campaign to produce results.

TIP: If you are spending money with a marketing firm, ask the following basic questions:

Have you worked in our industry before?

Will you produce the program content?

How long before we can get results?

What is the best way to build an audience?

How will you track leads?

How will leads be forwarded to the sales team?

What social media platforms would be most effective for our business?

How do you prioritize clients to meet deadlines?

Whenever you hire an outside resource, consultant, or vendor, make sure that the expectations are clearly outlined for both parties. Then hold the outside resources accountable for the results and deadline they said they would meet.

Your ROI for outside vendors should be measurable. Sometimes the return on investment will be the freedom to remove yourself from everyday work tasks so that you can work on your business rather than in your business. You should think of your time as a minimum billable amount of $500 to $1,000 per hour. The time you spend working on your business will reap much better rewards than doing manual tasks that may save you money but keep your business from growing.

Financial Ratios

Financial ratios or key performance indicators (KPIs) measure different financial aspects of a business. Financial institutions, stakeholders, and prospective buyers use KPIs to analyze credit worthiness, business health, and business worth. They are a great way to analyze what is performing well in the business and to determine which financial metrics a business should work on to improve performance. These ratios have more meaning when used to compare a company's performance with their competitor's.

The goal in providing these metrics is to help business leaders understand and be able to use the language that their banker uses. While they do not need to memorize these formulas, business owners do need to have a high-level understanding of what the metrics mean about business performance.

When outside parties, like bankers, financial institutions, and possible buyers look at these metrics, they are using them to assess the financial position of a company; outside parties use these metrics to determine bankability, financial soundness, and financial health.

Below are KPIs every business owner should know:

Current Ratio measures the overall liquidity of a company. Accounts listed in current assets should be collectable. The higher the ratio the better the company's ability to pay its debt and the more liquid the company. To calculate the current ratio:

Total current assets / Total current liabilities

For example, say a business has $250,000 in current assets and $100,000 in current liabilities. The current ratio for this company would be 2.5 and indicates that the company has enough cash flow to meet its short-term cash obligations.

Now let's change the example. Say the business has $100,000 in current assets and $120,000 in current liabilities. The current ratio for this business would be 0.83.

In this example, the company should be concerned that it may not be able to meet its cash obligations in the short term. This is when a business line of credit would be used to meet the business's short-term cash obligations.

Quick Ratio measures liquidity by only using cash and accounts receivable. The accounts receivable number should be reduced by any uncollectable accounts. The higher the ratio the better the company's ability to pay its debt and the more liquid the company. To calculate the quick ratio:

(Cash + accounts receivable) / Total current liabilities

Like the current ratio, if the quick ratio is less than one, the company has a cash-shortage problem and leadership should examine options to generate more cash.

Net Profit Margin

The net profit margin is an important business health indicator. It measures how much profit each dollar of sales generates.

Net profit before taxes / Sales

Business owners should compare their business net profit margin to their competitor's net profit margin. The higher the ratio the better. Specific industries will determine an acceptable net profit margin within that industry. The higher the margin the better the cash flow. Higher profits mean more cash in the bank before having to pay for debt on the books.

Accounts receivable days calculates the average amount of time to collect a credit sale. The lower the number of days the better.

(Accounts receivable / Sales) * 365

Strategies to improve collections and the results of this metric will be discussed in detail later in this book.

Accounts payable days calculates the average time it takes to pay vendors. It is used to gauge how a business is meeting its short-term obligations.

(Accounts payable / Cost of goods sold) * 365

This is the one metric that businesses do not want to have less pay days than their competitors. It indicates that the company is paying its bills to vendors faster than their competitors and not holding on to its cash for the longest time possible. Having less pay days on this metric versus competitors might mean the company is not managing cash correctly. This metric should only be lower than the competition if the company is taking advantage of a cash-discount payment program.

Inventory days calculates how quickly the company can react to market and/or product changes. The lower this metric the better.

(Inventory / Cost of goods sold) * 365

Every day that inventory sits on warehouse shelves costs money. In Chapter 8, we will be exploring strategies to get inventory-ordering processes right. Companies should at least be meeting their competitors' numbers on this metric.

Inventory turnover ratio tracks the number of times or cycles new inventory hits the shelves each year. In addition, it measures the liquidity of the product and the company's ability to effectively manage the stock. Turnover ratio is calculated as follows:

$$\frac{\textit{Cost of goods sold}}{\textit{(Beginning inventory + Ending Inventory) / 2}}$$

Inventory turnover measures how well cash and product purchases are managed. Turnover ratios vary by industry. A higher inventory number than industry standards could mean that the company's product is in demand and that there is a better cash flow than for competitors. This gives the company an edge over other businesses.

A lower-than-average inventory number may indicate a problem. This could mean too much product on the shelves. Slow inventory turnover can mean increased carrying costs for warehousing, insurance, and other holding costs. Overstocking inventory can also have an adverse effect on cash flow and create obsolete inventory.

Debt-to-equity ratio is a leverage ratio. It looks at liabilities of the company versus the equity in the company. Creditors want a lower ratio because it indicates lower financial risk.

$$\textit{Total Liabilities / Total Equity}$$

Investors want a higher ratio to realize a better return. The debt-to-equity ratio will also vary depending on the industry. In an industry like telecommunications, one would expect a high debt-to-equity ratio based on the amount of infrastructure expenses necessary to be successful in the industry. Cell towers and satellites are expensive.

Return on equity measures how much profit is being returned on investors' equity each year.

Net Income / Total Equity

For equity holders, the higher the return the better. Listen to the quarterly earnings reports on the news. Investors want a return for the money that they invest.

Return on assets calculates the company's ability to create profits with its assets; it indicates how many dollars of assets create each cent of profit. The higher this ratio the better.

Net income / Total assets

This metric measures how wisely a company spends cash in infrastructure investments, such as equipment, buildings, manufacturing plants, and so forth. A manufacturing plant would be expected to have more fixed assets investments than an IT service provider.

Gross fixed asset turnover ratio is used for companies that require a high amount of fixed assets. This is used in industries like an airline company that makes investments in purchasing aircraft or a transportation company purchasing freight trucks.

Sales / Gross fixed assets

The sales to gross fixed assets ratio calculates the multiple for annualized sales for each dollar of gross fixed assets it is producing.

Gross profit margin calculates the amount of dollars left to cover the company's fixed expenses. It shows the amount of gross profit generated for each dollar of sales.

Gross Profit / Sales

The higher the gross profit margin the better. Refer to Chapter Four for ways to improve gross margin.

EBITDA, "Earnings before interest, taxes, depreciation, and amortization," is the calculation of a company's cash flow generated from its operations. EBITDA is also a valuation method used to compare companies when involved in a sale or purchase. The higher a company's EBITDA number, the better the company's cash flow.

Debt leverage ratio calculates a company's ability to pay its debts from operating cash flow.

Total liabilities / EBITDA

If total liabilities exceed the company's cash flow, that does not mean that the company is bankrupt; it is a ratio to help investors and lenders determine the risk of the investment or loan. For example, if a business owner purchases a manufacturing plant, it is most likely that, in the beginning years, this ratio will be high. As long as the company can make the interest and mortgage payments from cash flow, they should be okay to take on the debt. Major purchases like this example should be reviewed by the CFO to make sure it does not put a strain on future cash flows and cash reserves.

TIP: You made it to the end. Great job. Please do not memorize these ratios. All you need to remember is if the ratio is good news for your company or if the ratio needs to be improved. It is only a snapshot of your financials for a period of time.

These ratios, like your financial investments, do not predict your company's future performance. You are in control of how your company will move forward. These metrics can be improved and a strategic CFO can help you develop a plan to improve your business financial health and increase profits.

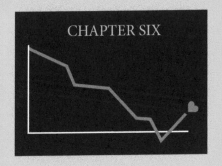

CHAPTER SIX

Score Big: Give Employees The Rules To Win

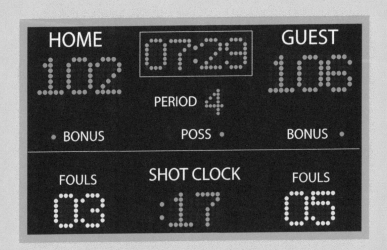

The biggest investment made as a business owner is employees. It is one of the most important aspects of profitability. Employees are the key to the company getting to the next level when scaling the business.

What is Employee Productivity?

Employee productivity is a hot topic for business owners, but how is it measured? We will explore several ideas to engage employees and measure employee productivity.

One of the key measures for employee productivity is sales per employee. This key performance indicator, or KPI, is used to measure the efficient use of resources: your employees. The theory is, the higher sales dollars sold per employee the more efficient the company workforce.

To calculate sales per employee, first calculate the number of full-time equivalent employees (FTE). For example:

ABC Company has thirty full-time employees who work forty hours per week and four part-time employees who work twenty hours each per week, totaling thirty-two FTE employees.

30 full time employees x 40 hours = 1200 hours
4 part time employees x 20 hours = 80 hours
1200 hours + 80 hours = 1280 hours
1280 hours / 40 hours per week = 32 FTE

ABC Company has annual sales of $5,000,000. To calculate its sales per employee the formula is:

Annual sales / # of FTE = Sales per employee
$5,000,000 sales / 32 FTE = $156,250

TIP: You may be asking yourself, now what? How do I use this number in my business?

This metric is an industry-standard number and used to compare similar businesses to each other. When you compare yourself to your industry, your sales per employee can tell you about the company differences.

If your sales per employee is higher than the industry, that means you are more efficient at utilizing your employees' time than your competitors are. If your number is significantly higher, it could indicate a potential problem. Ask yourself these questions to assess whether you are on track with your company vision and culture:

Is the quality of work produced by employees what I expect?

How long do employees stay at my company?

Would my employees recommend my company as a good place to work?

If the answers to these questions are no, you may be spending more money and resources on the back end of your business. This is not a good use of your cash and can be hurting cash flow.

You may be using your resources for production rework, new employee training, and hiring costs. All of these factors can increase your work costs overall and decrease your bottom line. Items that decrease your bottom line decrease the amount of cash available in your business.

Now let's say that a company's sales-per-employee number is lower than their competitor's. What does that mean? This could mean that the competitor has highly automated processes requiring fewer employees to manage the organization's infrastructure. It could also indicate that the employees are not producing that same quality of work as other companies. Maybe they are scaling up and their revenue is lagging behind the employee additions made for the predicted workload. These numbers can be improved by asking these questions:

- Are the processes repeatable for the business?
- Are the processes automated for better productivity?
- Does the employee count make sense for the amount of revenue the company is producing?
- How does the company's quality of work compare to the industry?

One of the businesses I worked with had a much lower sales-per-employee number than the competition. The owner thought this meant that she was overpaying her employees for the work they were doing. This could not have been further from the truth. Upon analysis of her company compared to her competitors, her competitors were much more automated than her company.

TIP: Do not jump to conclusions when looking at this number. Take a deeper dive into what the data is telling you.

By examining your sales-per-employee number, you will gain some valuable insights about your business and your competitors. I think, however, there is a better way to analyze how your employees help your business.

Employee KPIs

The notion that employees only need to know their job is outdated. When employees understand the company and department goals, they can get more things done in the business. Employee engagement is one of the keys to successful business performance. Employees today want to know how they contribute to the success of the business.

FAIL: Not sharing the company goals and initiatives with employees is a cash failure. When employees are kept in the dark, they cannot help the company reach its goals.

Imagine playing baseball and the teams did not keep score. What would be the motivation to score or play the game to win? Without a score, no one knows how they are doing. How do they know if they are playing a winning game for the business owner and the company? To play the game to win, company leadership needs to explain the rules of how to play the game.

Privately held businesses also want to safeguard their financial numbers. That is why they may have created an unintentional environment of secrecy. It is not necessary to have open-book management to create employee engagement. There are numbers that can be shared with employees without sharing detailed numbers and profits of the business.

Some numbers that can be shared with employees are sales and the company's gross margin percentage. These two numbers are where all the business's profits start. In fact, most employees already have an idea of what it costs to make product and the sales of the company. They do not understand all the other expenses that the business pays. These are the overhead expenses we discussed earlier.

Educating employees about the expenses that come out of gross margin, without disclosing actual numbers, goes a long way to helping them understand how the company uses profits from the sales of products.

Many employees do not understand all the expenses that a privately held business incurs after the cost of their product. Sharing information about company expenses helps employees understand that management is not a scrooge and hiding all the gold and profits for themselves.

Sharing with employees the company goals and how the company plans to achieve those goals gives employees insight into how they fit into the business. It is one of the first steps for employee engagement, to share how each department contributes to the profitability of the business and how each department is connected.

 **TIP:** When sharing company goals, emphasize how each department needs everyone to play their part in achieving those goals. Employees want to work for a successful company and help that company succeed.

Creating a Culture of Engagement

Some business leaders may think that sharing an annual performance review with an employee is motivation for success. It is really not the same thing, however, as sharing team goals. Helping employees learn to work together will create a culture of contribution.

Once company's goals are shared with the employees, how can the program's success be measured? Below are some things that are key to a successful program.

Create a scorecard

I encourage my clients to keep a scorecard for each department, then to share with the department managers and employees how their department scorecard helps the business achieve its goals. When creating employee KPIs, it is important that the KPIs have the following attributes:

Attainable goals

The metrics must be perceived as attainable by team members. It makes no sense to create metrics that cannot be completed by the team; it will have the opposite effect and will lower morale. What the company is asking employees to do should be in their skill set.

Visibility

The department goals must be visible to all team members. Goals can be posted on boards, televisions, or areas where everyone on the team can see their progress. To be effective these metrics must be updated in real time. Employees need to see how they are doing against the metric.

Quantifiable

The goals must be measurable. To have the right impact, the goals should be quantitative rather than qualitative; that is, goals should be measured in numbers, not quality. Employees must believe that they can impact and control the items being measured. Qualitative goals are subject to someone else's approval and not in the control of the employees being measured.

The rule of three

Limit the number of items being measured to a maximum of three key department goals for success. This allows employees to be laser focused on their goals. KPIs should not be a laundry list of projects or initiatives to be completed, which would be overwhelming for employees—or anyone. Limiting the amount of metrics to three requires the business leaders to be laser focused on how the department contributes to company goals.

Recognition

KPIs should be reviewed weekly with the team and successes should be celebrated. Team employees can be interviewed as to what improvements should be implemented for better team success.

Privately held companies that initiate a scoreboard for employees should encourage employee input. Employees are the best resource to improve business practices. They want their job to contribute to the company. This is true employee engagement.

Successful privately held companies use these strategies to encourage employee involvement:

Share goals

Leaders discuss company goals and initiatives at every level of the company. They share their vision with their managers, supervisors, team leaders, and employees. Employees need to understand how the company goals will benefit not only the company, but themselves.

Be visible

Leaders should be visible and available to employees. Employees look to leaders to set the tone for the day. If a leader walks into the sales pit with a scowl on their face, the sales team will think they have bad news. Remember, actions of the leadership team are watched by everyone. It is important that employees feel they can approach management with new ideas or problems they feel are preventing them from reaching their goals.

Show empathy

Leaders should listen to employees and value their opinions on how to improve company results. They should make sure employee ideas are acknowledged and not discarded at face value. Asking the following questions of employees can be used to clarify input:

- How do you picture that process working?
- How would this help you with your current responsibilities?
- What impact will this have on other team members?

 FAIL: Squashing employee creativity and ideas before the idea is explored and explained by the employee is a cash failure.

Many years ago, I worked for a business owner who did not understand why no employees came to him with ideas. Upon further exploration, we learned that he stifled ideas by doing one of three things when an employee approached with an idea. He would:

- Immediately respond "No"
- Tell the employee it had been tried before
- Say he would think about it but would never follow up

Needless to say, employees did not feel needed or heard. If the goal is to develop a team, this is the worst thing one can do. Employees will no longer come forward with ideas and managers will be setting themselves up to do all the work.

A better approach is to ask more questions and learn more about the employee's idea or proposal. If the idea does not seem feasible, then concerns should be explained to the employee, who may already have thought of solutions. Allowing the team to generate ideas will result in a culture of contribution.

Empower employees

When employees bring an idea forward, they should be given the latitude to work on the project. Management would be well-served to ask them to come up with a list of things they will need to make the project work. Can they investigate and develop the idea further? Will they make a presentation to team members? Empower them to be part of the process and success for their initiative. This will result in an engaged workforce and take the stress off leadership to come up with all of the ideas.

Still not convinced that this can help improve profits? Naz Beheshti, contributor to *Forbes*, in her article "10 Timely Statistics About the Connection between Employee Engagement and Wellness,[3] January 16, 2019, shared the following facts:

"Gallup found that highly engaged teams produce twenty-one percent greater profits than non-engaged teams." The study was based on employee behavior, not qualitative analysis. The Gallup report found that when employee engagement was made part of the strategy of the company, it increased the success of the organization. When employees are given clear expectations, the tools to be successful, and

---

3 Naz Beheshti, "10 Timely Statistics About the Connection Between Employee Engagement and Wellness," (January 2019), https://www.forbes.com/sites/nazbeheshti/2019/01/16/10-timely-statistics-about-the-connection-between-employee-engagement-and-wellness/#189460c722a0

support, they give the organization better work. Engaged teams in the top twenty percent of the study had forty-one percent less absences and fifty-nine percent less turnover than their counterparts.

Eighty-nine percent of HR managers agreed check-in and peer feedback were key for successful employee engagement programs. A recent report from globoforce.com[4] emphasized the importance of employee recognition and feedback. Like any good engagement program, the feedback and recognition should be tied to the organization's mission statement and core values. Employees want their work to have meaning and purpose. Employee engagement should be part of the fabric of the management team, not just a responsibility of the HR department.

Employees who feel heard are 4.6 times more likely to feel empowered to perform their jobs.[5] Recognition and feedback are not enough. Today's employee expects communication to happen in both directions. This Salesforce blog concludes that being heard is a larger push for equality and inclusiveness in the workplace. Companies with gender and ethnic diversity consistently outperform their competition, reaching more potential customers and incorporating a broader range of perspectives into their strategy and decision processes. Inviting more people to the table and ensuring their voices are heard is a win for everyone.

---

4 SHRM/Globoforce Survey Insights—Press Release (September 2018), https://www.globoforce.com/press-releases/globoforce-shrm-human/
5 Adam Kirsh, "Why Equality and Diversity Need to be SMB Priorities," (February 2018), https://www.salesforce.com/blog/2018/02/why-equality-and-diversity-need-to-be-priorities.html

Ninety-six percent of employees believe showing empathy is the key way to increase employee retention. Empathy is an essential part of emotional intelligence. Emotional intelligence is the ability to identify and manage emotions. A leader must be attuned to the emotions of others. Engagement and empathy are intertwined, and employees will not trust or respect an organization that does not show empathy.

Roberta Moore, an emotional intelligence expert, in her book *Emotion at Work: Unleashing the Secret Power of Emotional Intelligence,* says:

> *Empathetic leaders are viewed as approachable and authentic because their team feels safe sharing thoughts and ideas, and they care about their team's thoughts and feelings as much as they care about their own. Empathetic leaders satisfy their employees' human desires to feel heard and understood, leading to positive conflict resolution and gaining commitment to achieve goals.*

According to a brief by HR Dive[6], disengaged employees cost US businesses $550 billion a year. An exhaustive report titled "DNA of Engagement: How Organizations Can Foster Employee Ownership of Engagement" by The Engagement Institute, a joint study by The Conference Board, Sirota-Mercer, Deloitte, ROI, The Culture Works and Consulting LLP, explains the importance of engagement to an organization's bottom line. Most respondents knew why they were not fully engaged. They listed compelling missions, trusted relationships, and well-designed jobs as things they wanted leadership

---

6 Valerie Bolden-Barrett, Study: "Disengaged employees can cost companies up to $550B a year," (March 2017), https://www.hrdive.com/news/study-disengaged-employees-can-cost-companies-up-to-550b-a-year/437606/

to provide. The lesson here is that employees will say what they need to be engaged; managers just have to listen.

TIP: How can you tell if your employees are disengaged at your company? One way is to look at your employee turnover rate. The turnover rate is calculation is simple:

(Annual avg # of employees / # of employee departures) x 100

The higher this number the more costs you bear as a company for hiring, training, and lost productivity. On average it costs companies about $5,000 for each employee separation. Think of the impact this has on your company's bottom line and cash flow. Constantly hiring new employees causes a strain on your other employees and can create a stressful work environment. A stable engaged workforce will help your company reach its goals and help build your employee culture.

Creating employee dashboards is something that a strategic CFO can create. They can look at how departments interact, analyze what metrics can be improved to help productivity, and help teams be successful. Employee KPIs, like any metric, should be assessed for progress on a weekly basis. If the metric is not producing the desired results, it may need to be re-examined and adjusted.

As Jeanet Wade states in her book *The Human Team*, "I've seen businesses fail and I've seen them succeed. The common denominator in both cases - people! Let's face it: we're all in the people business.

When we meet people's needs and put them in the right settings, intrinsically our people can become excellent and can be nurtured to great individual, team-based, or organizational outcomes. Addressing human nature, meeting the needs of your people, and nurturing others begin with you, the leader, manager or facilitator. In our organizations, our people are our best assets."

Employees are the best resource to determine how to correct course and get back on track. Leaders should be sure to engage employees and reap the financial results for the company.

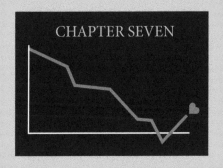

CHAPTER SEVEN

The Black Hole Called "The Balance Sheet"

The balance sheet is one of the most misunderstood reports for business owners and holds a wealth of information about the business. A picture of cash flow is not complete without looking at the balance sheet.

The balance sheet records all assets and liabilities of the company. It contains information about future cash inflow and future cash expenditures. The balance sheet is a critical portion of cash flow, which is often overlook by business owners. The report is written in accounting language, so it is hard for most business owners to understand.

 FAIL: Ignoring the information on the balance sheet that contains key information about the cash position of the company is a cash failure.

It is important for business owners to understand the three main sections of the balance sheet.

Assets are cash, future cash, long-term capital investments, or other investments the company has purchased or invested. Assets should be used to generate cash flow for the company. It is one of the key components of the balance sheet.

Liabilities are obligations that the company must pay to outside parties. Liabilities show where future cash payments must be made by the company that have not yet become due. They also show the company's long-term debt.

Owner's equity is the original cash investments made to start the company. This section of the balance sheet records distributions to the owners of the company. The difference between assets and liabilities equals the amount of owner's equity in the business. The goal is always to have a positive owner's equity, which means the business is profitable.

Current Assets

Current assets are assets that can be turned into cash in one year or less; they are considered highly liquid. Below is a breakdown of the accounts for current assets and the types of transactions found within these accounts.

- **Cash** is a liquid asset that is accessible immediately. These assets do not need to be sold to generate cash and include business checking accounts, savings accounts, and money market accounts.

- **Investments** are also considered liquid assets, but may require their sale, first, before cash is available. These include stocks, bonds, and mutual funds. Investments are used to increase the return on cash reserves.

- **Inventories** means product available for sale. The cost of inventory includes raw material and labor to manufacture the product. The cost of freight to bring the product to the facility and any other costs to deliver the product, such as import fees, can be included in inventory costs. These costs are kept in inventory until the product is sold to the customer.

- **Accounts Receivable** is the total amount of outstanding invoices that customers have been billed for the purchase of products and services. An invoice to a customer increases the accounts receivable balance. A payment decreases the balance and increases cash reserves.

Figure 6

ABC Company
Balance Sheet for May 13, 20XX

Assets
Current assets

a	Cash	$ 160,000
b	Investments	100,000
c	Inventories	250,00
d	Accounts receivable	500,000
e	Pre-paid expenses	20,000
f	Other	10,000
	Total current assets	**$1,040,000**

Fixed assets

g	Property and equipment	100,000
h	Leasehold improvements	25,000
i	Office equipment	5,000
j	Less accumlate4d depreciation	(50,000)
	Total fixed assets	**80,000**

Other assets

k	Goodwill	150,000
l	Startup costs	75,000
m	Less accumulated amortization	(40,000)
	Total other assets	**$180,000**
	Total assets	**$1,305,000**

Liabilities and owner's equity
Current liabilities

n	Accounts payable	60,000
o	Accrued wages	12,000
p	Accrued compensation	40,000
q	Income taxes payable	60,000
r	Unearned revenue	150,000
s	Line of credit	100,000
	Total current liabilities	**$ 422,000**

Long-term liabilities

t	Notes payable	$ 500,000
	Total long-term liabilities	**$ 500,000**

Owner's equity

u	Investment capital	50,000
w	Distributions	(100,000)
x	Accumulated retained earnings	433,000
	Total owner's equity	**383,000**
	Total liabilities and owner's equity	**$1,305,000**

- **Prepaid Expenses** are expenses that have been paid in advance of receipt. This could be deposits for rent, prepaid vendor invoices, deposits for utilities, or annual insurance premiums.
- **Other** is a category that represents miscellaneous expenses or losses shown on the income statement before they are deducted on the business's taxes. This category could also be revenues or gains that are not yet recorded on the income statement.

Fixed Assets

Fixed assets are assets that cost over a certain dollar amount and have a useful life of more than one year. Companies can set these limits. If the company sets the limit at $1,000, any asset purchase over this dollar amount, with a useful life of more than one year, would be set up as a fixed asset. You also may hear the term "capital investments" used or "infrastructure investments"; these are also fixed assets.

- **Property and equipment** could be a building, lift truck, vehicles, machinery to produce product, material-handling equipment and so forth.
- **Leasehold improvements** are physical changes or building upgrades to property not owned by the business. These upgrades become a permanent part of the building, such as offices, kitchens, lighting, roofs, and so forth. Companies cannot take these improvements with them.
- **Office equipment** typically includes office furniture, computers, laptops, servers, chairs, conference tables, et cetera.

- **Accumulated Depreciation** is used to account for the decrease in the value of assets over time. Depreciable items have a useful life over a period of years depending on the item.

Other Assets

Other Assets are assets that are not fixed and have a useful life of more than one year.

- **Goodwill** is used when a company is purchased. Goodwill is the difference between the purchase price of the company and the value of the net assets purchased by the new owner.
- **Startup costs** are costs associated with the start of a business. These costs include the business plan, research expenses, borrowing costs, organization fees, consulting fees, advertising, wages to train employees, and travel costs to secure vendors or distributors.
- **Accumulated amortization** refers to goodwill and startup costs, typically, which have a useful life of fifteen years and are amortized over this period. Amortization, like depreciation, is used to show the current value of the asset over a fifteen-year period.

Current Liabilities

Current liabilities are obligations that the company can pay off in less than one year. They are obligations that the business owes to vendors, state and government agencies, customers, employees, financing institutions, and company owners.

- **Accounts payable** tracks all outstanding vendor invoices to be paid, including company charge cards, invoices for inventory, rent, advertising, or any bill that has not been paid.
- **Accrued wages** are employees' wages that have been earned and not paid at the end of the accounting period.
- **Accrued expenses** include expenses that have been earned but have not been invoiced such as employee bonuses, commissions, vacation time, paid time off (PTO), and payroll taxes.
- **Income taxes payable** means the estimated amount of income taxes that the company owes at the end of the period being reported.
- **Unearned revenue** consists of customer down payments for items that have not been shipped or produced by the company. These prepayments are recorded as sales once the products ship or the service is performed.
- **Line of credit,** which every company should have, is used to cover monthly cash shortages. This account records the operating line of credit from the bank and the amount of credit that has been used by the company.

Long-term liabilities

- **Long-term liabilities** are obligations that take longer than one year to pay in full. These are typically loans, financing agreements, or other debt instruments.

- **Notes payable** denotes a loan or financing obligation that will take longer than one year to pay.

Owner's Equity

Owner's equity is the section of the balance sheet that records payments to owners, stock values, and the net assets of the company (accumulated retained earnings). Equity is the company's cumulative value at the end of the reporting period.

- **Investment capital** is the original or additional investments of cash used to start the business.
- **Accumulated retained earnings** shows the business's picture of financial health.
- **Accumulated retained assets** is the total assets of the company, less total liabilities.

By now you probably feel like a Wikipedia for the balance sheet. The real importance is to understand how all of this relates to cash flow and cash reserves.

How to Improve Cash Flow

Let's look at an analysis to help understand the ability to pay bills and generate cash. "Current assets" are liquid or can quickly be turned into cash. They show where future cash flows will be coming from for the company. For immediate influence on cash flow, a business owner should concentrate on the cash in the bank, accounts receivable, and inventory.

Accounts Receivable

The collection of accounts can greatly improve cash flow. Billing cycles and the timeliness of billing clients should be examined by the company. Delayed billings result in delayed payments.

 TIP: When I have worked with accounting departments and businesses in the past, they seemed to put billing on the back burner and enter vendor invoices before billing their customers. Stop this madness. You cannot pay your vendors without cash. You cannot collect on your sales unless you bill your customers. Invoicing customers should be your number one priority. Billing on time can have a dramatic increase on your cash flow.

In the construction industry, billing on time is one of the best strategies a business can use to improve cash flow. Many general contractors require subcontractors to bill monthly. If they miss the monthly cut off, it can delay payments from thirty to sixty days depending on the contractor and contract terms. The billing system used by the construction industry automatically delays payments with once-a-month billing. Missing the deadline could have dire consequences to the cash flow of the business. It is important to know the billing deadlines and meet them every month.

Big corporations can have payment terms sixty to ninety days and only process their invoices twice a month. Missing a deadline could extend cash flow another thirty days past the payment terms. Timely billing is critical.

 **TIP:** Here is another secret. Just because a business buys from you does not mean that you should automatically extend credit to them. Choose wisely before you decide to extend credit to a customer. Below are some best practices for offering credit.

Best Practices for Offering Credit

The first step to offering credit is to have a credit policy. The credit policy should include types of customers who will be extended credit. Knowing the answers to the following questions would be helpful:

- Will credit be extended to only businesses served on a monthly basis?
- Will a deposit be required for new customers or special orders?
- What is the minimum purchase required to be invoiced for payment later?
- Will invoices be due in seven days, fourteen days, thirty days, or more?
- How many years does the company need to have been in business to be extended credit?
- Does the customer have at least three vendor references?
- Does the customer have a bank?
- What will be the customer credit limit?
- What happens if the customer does not pay?
- Who pays if legal action is required?

Another best practice is to have a credit application. The credit application will include credit policies outlined above. In addition, the customer's credit rating should be checked with D&B, Experian, or Equifax, and vendor references should be called. Vendors will tell you if the customer is paying on time. They have no interest in helping a customer open a new account if they are not currently being paid. Checking references is important. References tell you in real time how the customer is paying.

FAIL: If you gave someone credit in the past and you are not being repaid, don't sell them anything else until you receive payment. Businesses wait too long before they stop servicing non-paying customers. Continuing service can affect cash flow and put the business in jeopardy. It is good business to tell the customer "No" and walk away. Remember, it is not a sale unless cash is collected.

Outstanding accounts, thirty days old or older, should be reviewed by someone on the team. A courtesy call to customers may ensure payments will arrive on time. Customers are less likely to take advantage and be slow-paying if they know they are being watched. Remember, the person calling will normally get paid first.

TIP: Make your customers aware that you take credit cards. Credit cards are convenient for customers and may help you get paid faster. A fee may have to be paid to the credit card company, but you will have almost immediate access to the funds. Ask yourself, is it better to be paid today or should I risk that I may not receive payment for thirty, sixty, or ninety days?

When transacting business with consumers, a company should consider asking for payment upon project completion. Plumbers, heating/air conditioning services, and others expect payment before leaving the consumer's residence. This policy saves time and improves cash flow. Many software applications accept credit cards and process services on employees' phones, tablets, or other electronic devices. A yard service, for example, may send invoices each month without automatic payments, but they also may spend many manpower hours chasing down payments.

If offering a monthly service, accepting payments by Automatic Clearing House (ACH), credit card, or setting up monthly automatic draws makes paying easier for customers and creates a steady cash flow each month for the business. No need to deal with checks and bank deposits.

Excess Cash Reserves

Excess cash reserves can make money for a business. The cash can be put in CDs or money market accounts for quick assess. Non-risk-averse companies can purchase mutual funds, stocks, bonds, or another investment to leverage the return on excess cash reserves. Business leaders are encouraged to see how to leverage this cash.

Accounts Payable

Bills that are owed to outside vendors are accounts payable. Paying bills to vendors as soon as received is not a good cash management system. Although companies are making suppliers happy with their promptness, they may be hurting their cash position in the short term.

When companies pay early, they are using cash for items that may not necessarily be critical to business that week. Cash for important payments, like payroll, rent, and insurance, should be considered before paying vendor payments. Paying bills early may prevent a company from taking advantage of other business opportunities if the cash is already used.

Managing when invoices are paid is as important as managing customer collection processes. Companies want to hold on to cash as long as possible. I recommend that they make it a policy to pay their providers when the invoice is due.

Some suppliers may offer cash discounts to pay an invoice within ten, fifteen, or twenty days. The invoice may state payment terms, such as two percent net ten. This payment term means, if you pay the invoice within ten days, the vendor will discount the invoice two percent of the cost. This is free money for the business and business owner.

For example, if the invoice is $10,000 and the invoice is paid within ten days, the payer would only pay the vendor $9,800. This saves the company $200 on the cost of the material or product. Make sure to pay these invoices early.

Many times, the vendor will require that payment is received by the tenth day of the month to take advantage of discounts. These discounts can add up over the year and reduce costs to the business. When possible, businesses should take advantage of cash discounts; it is free money that goes directly to the bottom line.

Vendors may offer various forms of payment, such as ACH payments, online payments, credit card payments, or other automated processes. These are all opportunities to hang on to funds until the due date of invoices and an effective way to manage cash more, as is automating monthly payments, such as phone bills, rent, and leasing agreements.

Local bankers or credit card companies may offer payment by virtual credit card. Instead of paying vendors by check, businesses use a virtual credit card number. Payment of invoices is approved just like it would be for a check run.

Once the payment run is approved, a file is uploaded to the credit card provider, who, in turn, sends payment to the vendor. When the payments have cleared, the payer then receives a detailed invoice showing all of the transactions.

For using this service credit card, providers pay a monthly rebate or cash reward. Local bankers or credit card providers qualify businesses for this method of payment.

Notes Payable

Debt is controversial for many business owners. Some brag that they do not have any debt and do not owe anyone. Although this may have been a good policy when the business was small, being debt-free sometimes makes it impossible to scale the company.

TIP: Debt, like taxes, can be a good thing. Yes, I am serious. Just bear with me before you tell me I am wrong. There is an "opportunity cost" when you do not finance certain transactions. For example, if you need a $100,000

machine and pay cash instead of financing, the transaction is the opportunity cost.

When you pay cash for the machine, $100,000 comes out of your cash reserves immediately instead of holding on to the money to be used for day-to-day expenses. What happens if you finance?

Say you finance the transaction for seven years at five percent interest. Your monthly payment would be $1,413.39 per month or $16,691 annually. This leaves you $83,039 in the bank to pay for other expenses. But what about the interest? Over the life of the loan, the interest would be $18,725. To finance per year would cost $2,675 per year. This is the price you pay to utilize another cash source rather than your working capital. Why is this important? You never know what is around the corner.

One of my clients was doing a big building move this year; they are debt-averse. They have good cash reserves, a line of credit, and no debt on their books. The move was going to cost approximately $400,000, between furniture, equipment, moving expenses, and office renovations. The owner wanted to pay cash because they had plenty of cash reserves.

This client had a good working relationship with their bank, and I encouraged them to finance these expenses rather than depleting their cash. They were dubious about the whole idea but reached out to their lending sources and secured two loans; one at 1.75 percent and another at 3.75 percent. They held on to their cash reserves.

Then the 2020 pandemic hit. The company was able to use the cash reserves that had been saved by the financing to pay their operating expenses. Had they used the money for the move and depleted their cash reserves, they would not have been in a good cash position. They owners were grateful that they had financed the moving expenses.

Retained Earnings

Retained earnings is one of the most important parts of the balance sheet. The net of retained earnings shows whether a company is profitable or not profitable. A company should always have more assets than it does liabilities; it is the sign of a healthy company that can pay its bills.

So far, we have discussed assets and liabilities on the balance sheet. The difference between assets and liabilities is called "retained earnings." Retained earnings is the actual value left in the company after everything is paid.

Negative retained earnings mean that the company's obligations exceed the incoming cash to the business. Negative retained earnings can be caused by:

- The owner taking more distributions from the company than the cash the company produces.
- The company has several years of losses.

Negative retained earnings can indicate that the company is not a viable business and may be in danger of bankruptcy. It is important for that company to figure out what is causing the negative retained earnings and correct course. One way to improve retained earnings is to invest more in the business.

FAIL: Investing in a business with negative profits and no plan to improve cash flows is a cash failure.

I have seen owners make the mistake of sinking all of their personal cash into a business to save it without making an action plan to improve business performance. This mistake can have devastating consequences for the business and business owner. If cash continues to be poured into the business without first analyzing what needs to be fixed, personal savings may be bankrupted. In this event, the first thing business leaders should do is figure out what is causing the company to report losses and then plot a course correction. Sinking more money into a business without a plan can bankrupt the business. Hiring outside help to create and implement a plan to improve financial results should be considered.

Let's get real. The balance sheet is totally confusing. It was the reason I flunked my first accounting class. Learning the balance sheet, literally, is learning a new language, so I encourage the readers not to be discouraged if they find this chapter confusing. The terms and meanings of the balance sheet take some time to get comfortable with.

TIP: Lean on your CPA, finance team, and strategic CFO to help decipher what is going on with your balance sheet. As you review your financial statements on a monthly basis, you will begin to understand this very important report.

CHAPTER EIGHT

Predict Cash Flow

Cash flow is the number one thing business owners need to understand about business. A company might make profits each month but be bankrupt by end of year. How can this happen? The company may have too much debt on its books, and the cash generated from operations may not be enough to sustain the company in the long term.

Debt is good, as long as it can be covered by the cash generated. How does a business owner know if they're generating enough cash to cover obligations?

 FAIL: Not understanding how much cash the business needs on a monthly basis to cover its fixed costs and debt obligations is a cash failure.

My first recommendation to clients is to start with a quarterly cash forecast for their company. This forecast will help them see the weeks they have a short fall. It will also serve to remind them of the important cash obligations they must cover, such as employee payroll and taxes.

The cash forecast is a simple cash budget that will show when expenses are due, when cash is expected to be collected from customers, and expenses for each week. Typical expenses should include are:

- Payments to vendors
- Payroll for employees
- General expenses, such as rent, utilities, internet service, advertising, telephone service, and business insurance
- Selling expenses, such as advertising, business meals and entertainment, marketing, commissions, and fees

- Guaranteed payments to owners
- Capital equipment and other capital expenditures
- Loan payments for operating lines of credit and debt service
- Tax Payments

Think of cash forecast as a profit and loss statement that includes your debt obligations' payments and collections on future assets. It pulls together balance sheets and profit and loss statements to assist business leaders in understanding their total cash picture.

TIP: Be detailed and realistic with your forecast. Do not over project your cash sales on a weekly basis. Be conservative. If you have accounts receivable over sixty days due, do not include these payments in your cash projections. To predict cash flows for future weeks and months look at your historical data and your sales plan. You can use your sales pipeline report to predict future cash flows and jobs based on probabilities.

The cash forecast is a cumulative picture of where future cash will be generated. It tells how the cash will be used in the future to cover obligations. The business owner can then make decisions about how to invest in programs for the company.

In a typical cash forecast, some weeks will show the company short on cash; other weeks will show the company over on cash. Over the quarterly thirteen-week period, the cash forecast should be positive. The exception to this rule is a seasonal business. With a seasonal business, it is important to have cash reserves set aside to cover negative cash months in the off-season.Cash shortages can also be covered by an operating line of credit. Remember, an operating line of credit is generally not approved when a company needs it; one must be set up when the business is working well. CFOs can help get this process set up with the business's bank.

Lines of credit are meant to cover the short-term cash obligations and not meant to be permanently drawn on. The proper use of a line of credit is to see the line go up and down.

For example, a company may be waiting for a client to pay their bill and may be short on cash for payroll. Say they use $30,000 of their line of credit to cover payroll on Monday. On Thursday, they receive $50,000 from the client. They should make a payment to their line of credit of $30,000 and put the $20,000 in the bank account. When a business pulls from the line of credit, bankers like to see the balance paid off even if the business pulls from the line of credit again in a day or two.

Lines of credit should not be used to purchase equipment. Banks and other financial institutions are happy to finance these types of purchases and will use the equipment purchased as collateral for the loan. This works just like a car loan. A business should have separate loans for financing its equipment.

Sources of Cash

What can a business owner do if they are not bankable? Their CFO can help them come up with strategies to reach out to other types of financing lenders. Banks are not the only organizations to approve loans. Below are other types of financing available:

Investors are outside sources from which business owners may be able to get cash infusion. There are different types of investors, all are interested in what kind of return the company can earn them for their money. Investors will want to look at the company's business plan, financial statements, and projected cash flow and growth.

Venture capitalists do not typically use their own money for investments. They are comprised of a group of professional investors who invest in rapid-growth companies that promise a high rate of return in three to five years. This is because only one in one hundred of their best investments will be successful. This makes them highly aggressive when looking at companies they are willing to invest in and will probably not be the best way for a company to seek capital unless they are in the technology sector. Venture capitalists tend to like investments of about $7,000,000.

Angel investors, unlike venture capitalists, may use their own money for investments. Angel investors are typically accredited investors and are similar to venture capitalists in that they are looking to invest in mostly startup businesses. Their goal is to get a high return on their investments, which tend to be smaller than venture capitalists' investments. Angel investors lean toward investing in business sectors they are familiar with. Having an infusion of cash can help companies reach their goals, but there may also be strings attached if an angel investor is used. Most angel investors will want some equity in the business, which may mean relinquishing control. Business leaders can expect an angel investment to be anywhere between $25,000 and $100,000.

Private equity firms invest in privately held businesses. Their goal is to buy and sell companies to earn a profit. Today, there are a lot of family firms that are classified as private equity firms. Private equity enterprises look to invest in businesses that they expect to have a high rate of return. Like venture capitalists and angel investors, their goal is to make money. Business owners must be careful about the deals with private equity firms and make sure that the deal made will benefit the business and help the business reach its goals.

Factoring companies prepay businesses money they expect to receive for their accounts receivable. The business actually sells their accounts receivable to the factoring company at a discount. Money is usually received quickly; there is no credit check nor lengthy financing process. The factoring company contacts the owing clients for collection of the payments. Generally, the advance will be ninety percent of the face value of the invoice plus a factoring fee of one to two percent for every week the invoice is unpaid. Some companies may also charge a processing fee of three percent. Using factoring companies is not a permanent solution to cash shortages but may work for businesses unable to get traditional financing.

There are two types of factoring: recourse and non-recourse. Recourse means the business owner assumes the risk if the customer fails to pay. This results in lower factoring rates for the business owner because the factoring company has less risk. If the invoice is unpaid, the company may be forced to purchase back the accounts receivable at full price plus the cost of the invoice factoring.

Non-recourse factoring means the factoring company assumes the risk. If a customer fails to pay, the factor is responsible for collecting. Non-recourse factoring has higher rates to the business owner.

TIP: It is important that you read the contract and understand the terms; you might find hidden fees. Make sure a financial professional and/or lawyer reviews the contract.

Invoice financing is typically done by a bank or financial institution at much lower rates than invoice factoring. A business's accounts receivable is used as collateral for an invoice financing loan. With invoice financing, the company is responsible for collecting invoices. Typically, invoices over ninety days are excluded from eligibility for the loan amount. A business can typically get a loan for eighty percent of the invoices total.

Merchant cash advance programs are generally used by businesses that have large amounts of credit card transactions; this may also be an option for short-term cash needs. Business owners can reach out to a credit card processor and find out if they are eligible for a loan. These loans typically have a flat non-refundable fee if the loan is paid off early. To repay the loan, the business owner commits to having a percentage of the business's daily credit card sales be used to repay the loan. PayPal offers a similar program, as does Shopify. Check with an e-commerce store to see if they offer merchant cash advances.

Typically, merchant cash advance loans must be paid off before the company is eligible for a second merchant cash advance. This type of loan can be a good strategy if the business does not have traditional accounts receivable and has not been able to obtain a line of credit from their bank.

Online Loans is a new way to get loans for businesses through online lending. Online loans have advantages. Most loans are processed quickly. Online lending sites normally have higher interest rates than a bank; a price paid for the convenience. Depending on the lender, a company can get term loans, lines of credit, SBA loans, invoice factoring, and merchant cash advances.

Grants are funding that a business receives for free. The grant does not require repayment to the granting agency, usually private organizations, non-profits, or economic development entities.

The first thing a company should check before applying for a grant is if they meet the requirements. The application process is often lengthy and requirements are specific for each grant. Because grants are a specialty, many business owners hire a professional grant writer to complete the application.

The SBA offers grants to business owners, who can find out if they qualify on grants.gov. State and local governments may also offer grant programs for businesses.

Pitch competition awards, like grants, are not required to be repaid by the winner. In pitch competitions, owners compete with each other to receive funding and free business advisory services. Many of these competitions are for startups, but others may be found for family-owned, minorities-owned, and women-owned businesses. Interested parties should check in their local regions and with national associations for pitch competitions in their area.

Family and friends often provide many businesses with startup cash. This is called "seed money." Family and friends can be great resources to help get the cash a business needs. It is important that these business transactions be documented. Friends and family need to understand that there is risk involved with the transaction: There is a possibility that they will lose their money.

A St. Louis woman reached out to friends when she started her restaurant. The friends loaned her money to help her get started. There was no documentation of the transaction. The restaurant became successful, and she reached back to her friends to return the money she had borrowed. But the friends wanted to be a part of the success of the restaurant and told her that their contributions were not loans, but rather investments in her business; i.e., they wanted the benefits of being owners rather than the repayment of their seed money. The restaurant owner, though, had no wish to have partners.

Needless to say, a legal battle ensued that cost the owner six figures in legal fees. The owner won her case, but was unable to open her second restaurant after using the capital in the business to pay her lawyers. She also lost a valuable friendship in the process. All of this could have been avoided if she had consulted an attorney upfront to draw up loan documents that clearly outlined the intent of the money the friends had provided.

 FAIL: Not getting the advice of experts when setting up transactions is a cash failure. In the above scenario, a loan document from an attorney would not have cost the business owner much. The money saved by not consulting a lawyer ended up costing the business owner hundreds of thousands of dollars. Remember, outside professionals help business owners mitigate risk and save money in the long run.

Other Options to Improve Cash Flow

When cash flow is insufficient to cover costs for a long period of times, a plan is needed. Financing will help to cover shortfalls, but is not a permanent fix for company cash flow issues. Part of having a healthy business is understanding what can be done to increase cash flows in the short term, to ensure that projections next quarter will be positive. If not, the cause of the negative cash flows needs to be found.

Below are good business practices that can help companies improve their cash flow. These strategies help to convert assets to cash or hold on to cash longer.

Increasing sales sounds simple, but it can be more difficult than one thinks. This strategy assumes that a business has
customers for the product in stock. Business owners should
make sure they have a good sales plan with clear-set objectives
and a good marketing plan to help acquire new customers.

Increasing sales works well for service providers or
business owners that have little cash outlay for new sales. For
companies with big cash outlays for new sales, this strategy
can make cash even tighter. It is important for businesses to
have a cash forecast to make sure that more sales will not
further strain their cash position. A strategic CFO can help
business owners put together a cash-flow plan.

The impact of a price increase will immediately increase
sales without putting a strain on cash. Remember, upselling
to current customers is easier than acquiring new customers.

Discounting and Sales can be a good way to generate
cash and move inventory. It can also be a great strategy for
low-priced retail items and may make sense if the business is
trying to get rid of slow-moving inventory.

Discounting high-priced items or luxury purchases may
devalue the business's brand. I encourage owners to understand what types of sales work best for their company and to
have a pricing strategy that is based on their marketing plan.

Business owners can also use this strategy to get rid of
obsolete inventory by offering it at a deep discount or at cost.
Unless inventory is turned into cash, it is a sunk cost and not
helping cash flow.

Make Informed Inventory Purchases based upon a review of what is moving quickly and what is moving slowly. I recommend that business leaders consider if they should order slow-moving inventory at all. Remember, inventory sitting on shelves is cash in the bank only if it sells it. Why re-invest in low-producers?

TIP: Make sure when estimating your inventory needs that you are being realistic in your forecasting. There is nothing worse than over purchasing a product and having no customers interested in buying it. Inventory is a huge cash eater. It is essential to get the amount needed correct, so that your cash reserves are not adversely impacted.

I have to admit that I like to watch "Shark Tank" on ABC. The "sharks" consistently ask entrepreneurs the same question: "How many purchase orders do you have for your product?" It is definitely a question you should be asking yourself. Be a good steward of your cash and buy what makes sense.

Just-in-time inventory system is an approach where inventory is ordered right before it is needed. This method is effective but requires a lot of knowledge and coordination with manufacturers' and suppliers' lead times, in addition to transportation time to the facilities. A just-in-time inventory system requires a detailed stocking and purchasing plan.

The benefits of a just-in-time inventory system is the use of cash. When used correctly, it can improve cash flow for the business. Just-in-time inventory utilizes the business's sales forecast and actual sales to determine the amount of inventory to purchase.

This inventory model can result in a business increasing its cash reserves.

Work with suppliers and vendors; negotiate discounts with suppliers based on the amount ordered. Discounts could also be based on bulk orders or the company's ordering statistics for the year.

Some business associations or trade associations offer bulk discounts to their members. Companies can also take advantage of prepaid freight and early payment cash discounts, or they can negotiate extended payment terms.

In the construction industry, for example, many contractors negotiate payment terms of paid when paid, which means that the subcontractor isn't paid until the general contractor is paid by the owner. This arrangement helps general contractors hang on to their cash. Subcontractors may negotiate the same terms with their suppliers.

If a business does have a cash-flow issue, they should not go radio silent with their vendors. Instead, they should call the vendor and make payment arrangements or let them know when they can expect payment. Most vendors will work with customers; they want to be paid too.

Delay capital purchases for equipment, vehicles, computers, or other infrastructure items; capital purchases use cash set aside to meet short-term obligations, such as payroll. Delaying capital purchases improves cash flow in the short term. Businesses should look at financing these purchases rather than using cash reserves.

Refinance term loans for longer periods to lower principal and interest payments for loan obligations, freeing up cash for other uses. The bank or financing firm will want to see that a company can make up its cash shortfall first. A CFO should be able to help put together a cash forecast.

TIP: Recently, at a book launch, I had a business owner ask me a very serious question. He wanted to know how to get through a difficult time in his business.

What do you do when you have everything on the line and things are not going well? You need to know your "why" and develop a cash strategy to get you through the crisis. Your why will help you make the hard decisions.

Getting up every day and hoping that things will get better is not a strategy. You need to put together a plan and implement it. Reach out to your management team and have them help you brainstorm on how to get things back on track. You are not in this alone. Your employees want the company to be successful. It is time to work on your business, not in your business, to turn the company around.

You have to look at your numbers and make the hard decisions. Your financial team and CFO can help you put together a plan to get back on track. The plan should include rebuilding cash reserves and company profitability.

What about when times are good? During those times, owners tend not to pay attention to their cash reserves and cash flows. But this is the most important time to do so. Having a plan for building cash reserves and investing excess cash is the key to success. Company executives should make sure cash is spent wisely. We never know what is around the corner. With cash reserves, businesses can weather times when business is not as anticipated.

CHAPTER NINE

Be a Planner, Not Dust in the Wind

Scaling a business without a plan is like setting the company adrift in the desert during a sandstorm. One of the first questions I ask business owners is where do they want to be financially in three to five years. In some instances, it has been a long time since the owner stopped the daily grind to assess what they wanted from their business. Here are some of the more common responses that I receive when I ask business owners where they want to be three to five years:

- Scale my business
- Retire and draw an income from my business
- Sell my business
- Buy a business
- Increase my profits to build personal wealth

All of these responses require a strategic plan. A strategic plan does not have to be a fifty-page document that is thrown in a drawer and never used again. It is a real-time plan that is adjusted as ideas and businesses change.

Starting with the financial goal at the end of the three- to five-year vision can help the business work backward to determine how to reach their financial goals. A strategic CFO will help the business determine sales, gross margin, and profits needed to attain long-term goals.

The Strategy Team

The business owner's financial goals do not have to be accomplished by the business owner alone. Reaching a financial goal quickly requires outside resources and business-team alignment. Below are key resources I recommend business owners invest in to reach their goals. This list is not meant to be all-inclusive, but meant to get business leaders thinking about who they need on their team for long-term planning. Based on the industry and company goals, other members may need to be added.

CFOs help the business owner organize the strategy team to ensure they understand the owner's goals for the company. It is important that everyone on the team understands what the owner wants to accomplish in the coming years. That way outside resources can align with each other to come up with the best plan to meet those goals.

Business attorneys are a key part of the advisory team. They can help with all types of legal documents regarding the company. The first thing a business attorney should review is the operating agreement or articles of incorporation and give any legal advice on how they should properly be written and filed.

A business attorney can help draw up non-disclosure agreements, non-compete agreements, intellectual property agreements, client contracts, and so forth. They can also protect the company's interest and help assess legal risks.

Estate attorneys will protect personal assets and help decide the best way to protect the business owner's wealth.

This can be done through many documents, including wills and trusts. An estate attorney should meet annually with the business owner to review plans and check for any changes in assets or beneficiaries.

Tax advisors work with business owners on tax-planning. A good tax advisor will be able to help with tax-saving strategies to defer or reduce tax liabilities for business and personal taxes. The tax advisor and CFO should be aligned with the company's three- to five-year strategy.

If the business strategy is to sell the business, the owner should reach out to a tax advisor and share this goal. When a business sells their company, there are specific tax-planning methods used to reduce the tax burden that a tax advisor can explain. The type of business structure, such as an LLC, C-Corporation, S-Corporation, partnership, or sole proprietorship, will have different tax consequences to the business owner. The structure of the business's sale also has specific tax consequences. It is important that business leaders consult a tax accountant who specifically deals in the sale and purchase of businesses. These strategies must be set up before the sale of the business. Some of them require a change in company formation, ownership, or the type of sale. Consulting the CPA can help business leaders get the most money from the sale of the business.

Wealth managers differ from financial planners. A good wealth manager will look at business and personal finances. They will give a complete picture of where the wealth is today and what needs to be done to accumulate wealth in the future. The process with a wealth manager should include review of the business portfolio, at least annually, to check if goals have changed and what life events may have impacted the plan.

Bankers come in different varieties. A business owner should have a good relationship with a commercial lender. The commercial banker can help get financing when the company is growing and the owner has plans for expansion.

An investment banker can help with outside financing or investments in the company. They can also help to buy or sell companies and raise capital by borrowing money or issuing stock. I advise my clients to have the appropriate banker on their team.

Insurance brokers help the company principals with commercial insurance, workers' compensation insurance, bonding, or other insurance requirements within specific industries. Insurance brokers have the ability to reach out to several insurance carriers to get the best price on business insurance. They should keep company leaders abreast of changes in industry practices to help the company insure against risk.

CPA firms, besides helping prepare company tax returns, should be able to issue outside annual company reports: audits, reviews, and compilations.

Audits require a CPA firm to examine the company in depth. The CPA firm will request certain information from the business, such as accounting records, account reconciliations, and business formation documentation. They review a company's internal controls and verify account balances. An audit is the highest form of financial-statement review, in which the auditor is asked to give an unqualified opinion on the condition of the company books. The best opinion is one which indicates that the company has clean books.

The CPA firm provides a detailed analysis and assurance regarding the reasonableness of the financial statements. Financial reviews do not include testing of the books or the use of outside parties to confirm company balances.

The CPA firm performs compilations where it assists the company in putting together financial statements. A compilation does not require the CPA firm to provide assurance that there are not material modifications to the financial statements. This is the least expensive type of service and may satisfy outside parties such as bonding and insurance companies.

Annual meetings should be held, at a minimum, once a year between business owners and their strategic team to review the company's three- to five-year strategic plan. This allows the experts to bounce ideas off each other to come up with the best plan for the owner and the business. Annual meetings place everyone in the same room to hear the same thing at the same time and avoid wasting time talking to each advisor individually.

In addition, advisors can ask each other direct questions about the suggestions made, removing the owner from the position of mediator. When advisors know the goals, they help to achieve them. It is amazing what can be accomplished when everyone is on the same page.

TIP: How much more personal wealth and business valuation can you attain by setting up this annual meeting? So often, I meet with business owners when they are ready to sell. They have not had these conversations with their advisors and do not understand the necessary planning needed to obtain their sale price. Imagine the power of starting these conversations today and how much more you can leverage your business value and personal investments.

You need to find the balance between re-investing in your company and creating your personal wealth. It is okay to take planned distributions from your company and build wealth outside of your business.

How to Plan

Everything in the business plan starts with the business owner, who controls where they want to be in three to five years. No one can answer this question for them. Owners may need to reflect on what they want to accomplish. What is it that they are creating for themselves, their families, their teams, and/or their investors? Here are some questions I propose that my clients ask themselves to start them thinking strategically about their businesses:

- Where do I want my business to be three to five years from today?
- Do I want to build a company in order to sell it later?
- Do I want to transfer wealth to my family?
- What is my main reason for having my business?

- What do I want my personal life to look like three to five years from today?
- What does my company do well today?
- Where do I see room for improvement?
- Do I want to retire and draw an income from my business?

One-Page Strategic Plan

Business owners can start the journey with a simple one-page strategic business plan, which focuses on the big picture and organizes thoughts about the organization.

"Our Company" Vision.

The first section of the one-page strategic business plan is all about the company and includes the company vision, the company mission, and its core values. The vision should be able to answer the below questions when a customer is researching companies to do business with. The questions are meant to help business owners to think through one-page strategic business plan sections.

- What do I want the company to achieve?
- What is my vision of the company three to five years from now?
- What is the "why" behind the company and in everything I do?
- What is the Simon Sinek Golden Circle?
Mission.

The company mission statement explains the what and how of the company. It answers these questions:

- What drives us as a company?
- How do we work?
- What do we do?
- What makes us different?
- What do our customers think we do best?
- What do we want to make sure that customers know about us as a business?
- What is our unique selling proposition?

Core Values.

Core values are all about the integrity of the company and how it will do business with others. Business owners should consider the following when creating the company's core values:

- What are the principals our company will use when working with customers and employees?
- How will the company conduct itself in business?
- What types of behavior are expected of employees when working with customers?
- How will the company work with outside parties?
- What are factors the company thinks are important when conducting business?

Goals

Obstacles. I encourage business owners to ask themselves, "What is keeping me from reaching my goals today?" These obstacles are barriers to success. When owners think about obstacles, they should consider the impact of the following items on the business:

- Cash
- Lenders
- Sales
- Profits
- Technology
- Staffing challenges
- Taxes
- Regulations
- Industry changes
- Lawsuits
- Other Concerns

Figure 7

One Page Strategic Plan	
Our Company	
Vision	Where should the company go and why?
Mission	who we are, what we do, how we work, what makes us different.
Core Values	Your work compass of principals and how the company will operate.
Goals	
Obstacles	What is preventing us from reaching our goals?
Long-Term Goals	Where will the company be 3 to 5 years from now? Sales, profits, employees
Short-Term Goals	What are the company goals for the next year?
Measurement of Success	Sales $$, # of customers, % of profits, # of employees?
Strategy	
Resources Needed	How will the infrastructure be set up to succeed?
Financing	What are the business financial needs? What are the sources of income?
Plan Launch	How will the plan be presented to the team and launched for the company?
Progress	Assess progress, measure results, re-assess and implement changes.
SWOT	
Strengths	Internal strengths that the company controls, like customer service or branding.
Weaknesses	Internal weaknesses that the company controls and can improve on a regular basis.
Opportunities	External factors not controlled by the company, such as innovation and technology.
Threats	External factors not controlled by the company, such as regulations and import fees.

Long-Term Goals

These are goals three, five, or more years away in the long-term vision; they should be big. To be successful, they should push past preconceived limits. It is amazing what one can accomplish when thinking bigger.

 TIP: Imagine sales numbers three times bigger than you are considering right now. What could you accomplish for your customers, your employees, and your family? Make sure to set measurable goals for the business and yourself.

Below are some items business owners should consider when planning for their long-term goals:

- Annual sales number
- Revenue streams
- Profits
- Number of employees
- Number of customers
- Company brand and reputation

Short-Term Goals

Short-term goals should be aligned with long-term goals. I encourage my clients to think of how they can move their company forward in the coming year and make progress toward their long-term goals. Moving fast by quickly implementing and working a strategic plan is the quickest way to achieve a goal. If goals are too small from year to year, business owners will set themselves up for failure. Short-term goals should stretch company leaders and employees to think

bigger. Like long-term goals, short-term goals should be set up and measured by:
- Annual sales number
- Revenue streams
- Profits
- Number of employees
- Number of customers
- Company brand and reputation

Measurement of Success.

Goals that are not measured, do not happen. Remember, the most successful plans make sure that goals are quantitative not qualitative. Business leaders should determine what measurements will be used to measure success. These goals and the items measured may change over time. Being consistent and re-assessing the measurements for success will help keep businesses on course with their big picture vision.
- Number of new sales
- New revenue streams
- Increased profits
- Additional employees
- New customers
- Lead conversions
- Other measurements determined by goals

Strategy

Strategy helps to determine how to accomplish goals; it is the secret sauce. Strategy provides a roadmap to success and helps adjust plans where needed.

There are four categories in the strategy section of the one-page strategic plan. "Resources Needed" focuses on how the company needs to be organized to succeed. "Financing" focuses on how cash will be generated. "Plan Launch" is the implementation of the plan. And, finally, "Progress" is the measurement and assessment of the progress toward the goal.

Resources needed

When considering the resources a business owner will need, they should assess how technology can help accomplish their goals.

- Is there software that will help automate processes in the business?
- Can software help free up a team's time to do other revenue-producing tasks?
- What are the resources the team needs to reach their goals?

A company's organizational chart should be detailed. Business leaders should sit down and draw out what staff will look like for the company, listing positions and what they do. The below questions will help to complete this task:

- Who will be the key employees or department heads?
- How many employees will report to them?
- What are the department names and responsibilities?

TIP: Visualize the team. You want to build a team that can handle the business without you being in the picture all the time. This allows you to start reaping the benefits of being a business owner. It gives you the freedom to start working on your business rather than in it. You are the thought leader, driving the business to reach whatever goals you set out for the company.

What other resources will your company need to achieve its goals? Think about logistics, operations, warehousing, sales, human resources, and marketing. How will they be different than they are today?

Financing

When businesses have rapid growth, cash becomes a problem in the business. Typically, business owners in a rapid-growth cycle find themselves constantly short on cash because as soon as they receive payment the cash is out the door to cover expenses.

There are several ways to finance this shortage, that is, via the use of investors, debt financing, or a lender or bank. An outsourced CFO can help determine how much cash will be needed to expand and can help explore options. Many of these options are discussed in Chapter Eight under "Sources of Cash."

Plan Launch

The plan launch is where all the action happens. This is where the business owner presents the plan to the team and gets their buy-in. Employees should be actively involved in this part of the plan and understand the metrics, goals, and deadlines needed to be met to be successful.

Prior to the plan launch, company leaders should share with their team the big-picture vision; they should explain their vision, company mission, and core company values. They should ask employees how they feel about where the company is headed and where they feel they can contribute to the company's success. Plans that come from the top down can be met with resistance, so involving employees in coming up with plans gets them involved and shows them first-hand that their contributions to the team are valued.

Brainstorming sessions can be instituted to discuss implementation of ideas. Even better, teams can be encouraged to come up with milestone plans to execute the company's initiatives. It is easier to help people be successful when they are in charge of their work. The team was hired to help; business owners do not have to have all the ideas. Employees should be allowed to help expand on dreams.

TIP: Employees should understand what the rewards will be for them. Will they earn more time off? get a bonus? go on a company-paid vacation? How will they benefit from helping the company reach its goals? Share the big picture and let them know how they will be rewarded for their hard work.

Progress

Progress is where most plans fail. This is the measurement of company results. To make progress, business owners have to consistently measure results. The results will tell if the company is on track or off track on the goals it has set.

If the company is off track, an action plan should be made by the team to correct course and get the company back on plan. Re-assessing progress and implementing changes are the keys to success.

The plan launch is not going to be perfect. It is meant to be a starting point to help a company reach its goals. As the plan launch progresses, the team will think of better ways to do business and help make changes that will have positive impacts for the company. To take full advantage of a team's resources, business leaders should take the time to be seen and listen to employees' concerns and suggestions. Employees know how to make their jobs more efficient if given the chance. If company principals help them develop new ideas, they will have a team engaged and willing to make changes happen.

SWOT

SWOT is an acronym for "strengths, weaknesses, opportunities, and threats." A SWOT analysis should be conducted by a business at least once per year. The SWOT analysis will change based on many circumstances and can affect the company's goals and strategic plan.

Strengths strengths are the internal strengths that the business owner controls. This could be the excellent customer service provided or brand recognition. It could be the company's why.

Weaknesses are also controlled by the company principals. This means that it is in their control to come up with plans to improve weaknesses. Team members and customers can be great resources to determine company weaknesses, and the company should be continually working on improving them.

Opportunities are external factors that are not controlled by the company. This could be innovation in the specific industry. For example, the printing industry has change in the last fifty year. Changes can be driven by technology advancements or a competitor going out of business. Business owners should be on the lookout for opportunities; they can generate new revenue streams and change operations to improve strengths.

Threats, like opportunities, are external factors that are not controlled by the company. Threats could be new tax laws that increase the company's tax burden and decrease profits. They could be a newly imposed import tax that dramatically effects pricing, like the steel import tax imposed on steel in 2018. Maybe it is a pandemic that has shut down the economies of the world. Threats like these are out of the company's control but must be addressed in the company's strategic plan.

A SWOT analysis is a great exercise to engage a team. It can help identify what the company does well and where employees can help improve company performance. A SWOT analysis done prior to goal-setting can help identify obstacles that are preventing the company from achieving their goals. This tool can help analyze progress and reassess what is necessary to achieve goals.

TIP: Your strategic plan is not a one-and-done document. The one-page strategic plan is a great framework to outline the big initiatives for the year. You can also use it to outline what you want to accomplish each quarter in your business. Breaking these goals into bite-size pieces and assigning team members to implement them will help you make faster progress. Giving team members and managers responsibility will help toward achieving your goal of working on your business rather than in it.

What can you picture yourself doing in your free time? Do you want to travel? Is there something on your bucket list that you want to accomplish? Do you want to relax and enjoy time with your family? Whatever your goal, make sure that it is part of your everyday mantra See yourself visibly doing the activities that you aspire to do each day. It will help keep you focused on your goals.

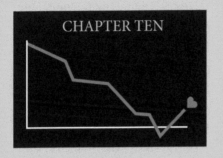

CHAPTER TEN

Myth Buster – Understand the Monthly Facts

This last chapter deals with practicing what you have learned and putting everything together so you can focus on a plan for you and your business. If you're like me, when you are learning anything new, it is helpful to have someone put all the pieces of the puzzle together.

Your books need to be closed every month by a financial professional on your team. This can be an outside resource or an internal finance team member. Your books should be closed on the same day every month—I typically recommend by the tenth. When you start closing at a date later than the tenth, financial information is delivered too late to make an impact on the performance of the current month.

Someone who has a deep understanding of accrual basis accounting should review your financial statements for accuracy. This can be a financial manager on your team or an outside resource, such as a strategic CFO. These individuals will ensure the complete reconciliation of bank accounts, charge cards, and balance sheet accounts.

Your balance sheet and income statement are dependent on each other to produce accurate financial statements. If the balance sheet is incorrect, the information on your income statement is also inaccurate.

Get your monthly facts and review your financial numbers with your financial professional. Ask questions about items you do not understand or that look off to you. Make sure that the team understands what items are in each line of your statements.

Budgets Versus Forecasts

If financial statements report the past, what is used to reach future goals? Many business owners are familiar with a budget. Budgets are completed once a year and, in my opinion, for a rapidly growing business, obsolete by the end of month one or month two. Budgets and variance reporting work well for businesses that have no desire to grow or improve. They are static documents that do not follow the ebbs and flows of a business making huge growth-strategy decisions.

What I believe business owners should utilize is a twelve-month rolling forecast. A twelve-month rolling forecast continually looks ahead twelve months to predict what needs to be done for the business to reach its financial goals. It predicts the company creation of cash and shows how cash will be used in the coming month.

The key to a successful twelve-month rolling forecast is to adjust numbers for what has gone right or wrong in the forecast monthly. Say, for the twelve-month forecast, a company picks up a major client, worth $500,000 to $1,000,000, that blasts through the original sales forecast number. The company would want to adjust the sales forecast to reflect this new revenue and increase sales goals for the year. Remember, if a business is in growth mode, they are all about stretching themselves.

In addition, they will want to examine what additional resources will be needed to fulfill this new major client's order. Do they need more staff, warehouse space, or production time? They should look at the expenses associated with the sale and adjust their forecast accordingly.

A budget would take this as a win without getting the business owner to think more analytically about the financial expenses associated with the sale. This sale causes expense numbers to increase. The forecast will capture expected expenses and point out any deficiencies or wins with the plan.

Forecasting involves a team, and the team needs to understand the part they play in the finances. I am not advocating open-book management, but I do believe managers need to understand the forecast for their departments, including labor costs. Providing a clear picture of financial expectations for the management team and receiving their input will allow management to have a much more meaningful financial plan.

Forecasting should not be limited to just the income statement. Business leaders should also look at financing needed to accomplish goals, fixed asset expenditures, debt obligations, owner's payments, and other balance sheet items that affect cash flow.

Cash Flow Statement Versus Cash Forecast

A cash flow statement is one of the three major reports that should be included in a financial package. The cash flow statement combines the income statement and balance sheet to show the history of how cash was used in the business for the month. Items that have a positive balance produced cash; items that have a negative balance used cash. A strategic CFO will be able to help business owners understand the report in more depth if needed. Some of the more common uses and sources of cash will be highlighted in the cash flow statement.

The cash flow statement is divided into four main categories: operating activities, adjustments to net income, investing activities, and financing activities.

Operating activities

The cash flow statement starts with operating activities. The cash for the month will be generated from the net income the company reported on their income statement. The next step is to add back or deduct items that will not generate cash or will use cash for the month.

When using the accrual basis for accounting, the cash flow statement converts the company books back to the cash method to determine whether cash increased or decreased for the period and how the cash was used.

The following activities increase cash reserves for a company:
- Positive net income for the period
- Collecting payment on outstanding invoices
- Selling inventory
- Paying accounts payable on the due date
- Delaying payment of bills
- Acquiring new loans or draws on lines of credit
- These activities decrease cash reserves for a company:
- Negative net income for the period
- Increases in accounts receivable outstanding
- Purchases of inventory

- Payment of loans and reductions in lines of credit balances
- Purchases of fixed assets

Figure 8

ABC Company Cash Flow Statement	Dec 20XX
Operating Activities	
Net Income	260,000
Depreciation	10,000
Adjustments to Net Income	
Accounts Receivable	(45,000)
Inventory	(65,000)
Other Current Assets	5,000
Accounts Payable	(10,000)
Other Current Liabilities	2,000
Total Adjustments to Net Income	**(113,000)**
Total Operation Activities	
Investing Activities	
Fixed Asset	60,000
Total Investing Activities	**60,000**
Financing Activities	
Long Term Liabilities	(36,000)
Total Financing Activities	**(36,000)**
Net Change in Cash for Period	**181,000**
Cash at Beginning of Period	200,000
Cash at End of Period	381,000

In Figure 8, the ABC Company made a profit of $260,000. Once the adjustments were completed to net income, the company had another $181,000 in cash reserves to add to their cash balance. This resulted in an ending cash balance of $381,000 for the year.

A common question for business owners is what is the correct amount of cash reserves for my company? This question is complicated to answer. It depends on the availability of funding to the company, the amount of debt on the books, and monthly operating expenses. It also depends on the industry and the net profit margins that the company generates.

By holding the right amount of cash reserves for the company, at a minimum, they should be able to cover their short-term needs.

Cash reserves for a seasonal business will be different from a business that has reoccurring monthly income. Cash reserves for a highly leveraged business will be different than a business that specializes in consulting services. A strategic CFO can help a business owner to determine their cash needs.

Let's review the levers that help to increase profits and provide more cash to create cash reserves for a business. Businesses must have sales to generate cash; sales numbers drive the profits of the business. To create a winning sales plan, a business owner needs to:

- Hold their team accountable for sales goals
- Create weekly activity number metrics for the sales team to meet

- Create a commission plan that rewards the sales team and drives the desired sales for the team to meet
- Create a sales pipeline to track deals and estimate future cash flows

The price for products and services determines the profitability of a company—if the right pricing structure to generate positive cash flows and cash reserves has been put into place. To ensure the right pricing, managers need to:

- Determine the breakeven point for the company
- Evaluate whether the company can generate enough sales to hit the breakeven point
- Initiate an annual price increase for the company
- Develop a strategic pricing model to eliminate unprofitable business
- Focus on higher margin products and services

Business owners should know their company's gross margin and compare how their company measures up to the competition. The goal is to improve gross margin and net margin for greater cash flow. To improve gross and net margin, business owners should:

- Examine the elements of the cost of goods sold for savings in price and labor.
- Eliminate company waste
- Automate company processes
- Review company expenditures for possible cost savings

Numbers people are an important part of a team. Having the right team players will help a business analyze their financial results in the following ways:

- Accrual-basis accounting helps to match revenue and expenses to determine the business's profitability.
- Return on investments (ROI) can be used to determine the appropriateness of the company's uses of money.
- Financial ratios are used to determine the current economic health of a company.
- A strategic CFO is an important part of a finance team.

Employee engagement and culture will create better profitability and cash flow for business. Strategies include:

- Getting employees involved in business improvements
- Creating a scorecard for teams so they can contribute to the profitability of the company.
- Listening to employees and developing them, which will decrease company turnover and improve overall operations.
- Remembering that the proof is in the numbers.
- And remembering, millennials are smart, tech savvy, and attuned to looking at how they fit into the big picture.

The balance sheet is the report with all the action. It tells the story of future cash flows and expenditures that will be required by a company. The balance sheet and the income statement are married to each other; that is, if either statement is incorrect, then the financial reports are all incorrect. Both must be accurate for the business to have a clear accounting of its financial picture. Business owners should understand that:

- Assets are used to finance loans for the company.

- Lines of credit are a good use of funds to cover short-term cash obligations.
- Balance sheet accounts can be used to strategically improve cash flow.
- Customers who receive credit should be chosen wisely.
- Debt used strategically can be a wise way to ensure the company has cash reserves.
- Owners want to realize a return on their investments.

Every business should forecast cash, at a minimum, thirteen weeks into the future. It is recommended that larger companies and seasonal businesses look at the cash forecast on a twelve-month basis. I advise my clients to:

- Be aware of the many sources of cash for the business, from financing to investors to grants
- Develop a strategy to increase cash flow
- Understand the amount of cash needed to support growth and operations

Strategic planning will stretch a company and help it get to the next level of business. Business owners should:

- Develop a strategic team of advisors to help reach their goals
- Hold an annual meeting with advisors to get advice from the experts
- Develop a one-page strategic plan to achieve their goals
- Engage employees to help implement the plan

All of these things help get a business to the next level.

Here is how I recommend that you start: Know where you are financially today. Your team should be able to issue monthly statements for your review. If they are having difficulty, it is time to call in an expert for help. A strategic CFO can help analyze what is going on and implement changes to get the team back on track.

Evaluate the financial position of the company today in comparison to your big picture vision and strategic plan. When developing your strategic plan, start with the company, vision, mission, and core values. Then I recommend doing your strengths, weaknesses, opportunities, and threats (SWOT) with your management team.

The SWOT will help you identify areas that need to be improved in your operations and help you determine your next steps. Your sales, marketing, pricing, and employee engagement will all be part of your plan implementation. A strategic CFO can help you put together a financial plan for three to five years that includes pricing structures, overhead costs, revenue streams, and the other operational changes.

Once you have your plan determined, bring together your success team to brainstorm about how they can help you reach the big picture vision. They can also help you strategize to remove obstacles that may be getting in your way.

Implement your plan and be consistent in measurement, assessment, employee engagement, and course corrections. Planning assessments and re-assessments will guide your company toward your goals and help you succeed.

To achieve goals, make sure to have a strategic CFO assess the cash needs and financing options available to the company. This forward thinking and implementation will help to increase cash reserves for the company and also help you build personal wealth.

When you became a business owner, you knew that it would not be easy. It has taken grit and hard work to get your business where it is today. You can go so much further with the right financial partners at your side and a monthly review of your finances. Imagine having enough cash reserves to get the company to the next level. Cash gives you the flexibility and time to make decisions in impossible situations, like a pandemic—a threat that no one ever saw coming.

Cash reserves and profitability to create cash reserves allow you to think of the possibilities and work on your business rather than in your business. And you can operate your business in confidence rather than in fear. Success is at your fingertips with the right amount of cash and a good plan. Building personal wealth is an essential part of that plan. You do not want to end up the way my grandfather did. He worked his entire life and had nothing to show for it at the end. He was broke at the time of his retirement.

Stop paying yourself last and putting the daily activities of your business first. Set aside planning time once a week to make progress on your business goals. This time should be non-negotiable; it is your time to work on you and your business.

Only you can make your goals happen. You have to be able to make the tough decisions and move on from business missteps. For some of you, looking at your finances and facing your reality today can be a scary proposition. The simple truth is you cannot move forward without knowing where you are.

No matter where you are today, it is just the starting point to reach your ultimate goals. Start working on your vision now. Do not let your Frankenstein keep you from your Einstein. Get out of your way and out of your head. Take action today to reach your goals.

Recently, I heard a survey of people that had just turned eighty. When asked what they most regretted in life, the answer was the same: They regretted not taking some of the risks that they had faced in their lives because they will never know the outcome.

Knowing your financial position and taking calculated risks is the true road to success. Live your life now with no regrets. Start making your business the success you have always envisioned and make sure you get the help of experts along the way.

About the Author

Debi Corrie is the owner and CEO of Acumaxum, a strategic CFO company dedicated to helping business owners increase cash, maximize profits, and scale their businesses. A dedicated and thoughtful business strategist, she owns multiple businesses and is dedicated to helping all business owners achieve financial success.

Combining a strong financial acumen with operational expertise, Debi quickly identifies business objectives, forges ambitious development strategies, and transforms challenges into robust growth opportunities. Collaborative and confident in her approach, she creates authentic, inclusive work cultures which drive ownership, accountability, and a crucial competitive advantage.

Debi received her Bachelor of Science degree in business administration with a major in accounting from the University of St. Louis while working full time. She is a CPA, CGMA, and a member of the American Institute of Certified Public Accountants (AICPA), the National Association of Tax Professionals (NATP), and the Association for Corporate Growth (ACG). She is a mentor for Parkway Spark, a past board member for the Professional Women's Alliance of St. Louis, and past board Member for Inventors Association of St. Louis. As a member of the National Speakers Association (NSA) of St. Louis, Debi speaks publicly on a variety of topics, educating her audiences on how to intertwine numbers and people for successful business outcomes.

Facebook: https://www.facebook.com/Acumaxum-102399371627544

Twitter: https://twitter.com/Acumaxum

LinkedIn: https://www.linkedin.com/in/debicorriecfo/

Instagram: https://www.instagram.com/acumaxum/

Bibliography

Beheshti, Naz, "10 Timely Statistics About the Connection Between Employee Engagement and Wellness" (January 2019), retrieved September 30, 2020, from https://www.forbes.com/sites/nazbeheshti/2019/01/16/10-timely-statistics-about-the-connection-between-employee-engagement-and-wellness/#189460c722a0Bolden-Barrett, Valerie, Study: "Disengaged employees can cost companies up to $550B a year" (March 2017), retrieved September 30, 2020, from https://www.hrdive.com/news/study-disengaged-employees-can-cost-companies-up-to-550b-a-year/437606/

Kirsh, Adam, "Why Equality and Diversity Need to be SMB Priorities" (February 2018), retrieved September 30, 2020, from https://www.salesforce.com/blog/2018/02/why-equality-and-diversity-need-to-be-priorities.html

SHRM/Globoforce Survey Insights—Press Release (September 2018), retrieved September 30, 2020, from https://www.globoforce.com/press-releases/globoforce-shrm-human/

Sinek, Simon, "How great leaders inspire action" (September 2009), retrieved September 30, 2020, from https://www.ted.com/talks/simon_sinek_how_great_leaders_inspire_action

"Survival of private sector establishments by opening year," (Rep. No. Table 7). (n.d.). Retrieved September 30, 2020, from Bureau of Labor Statistics website: https://www.bls.gov/bdm/us_age_naics_00_table7.txt

CPSIA information can be obtained
at www.ICGtesting.com
Printed in the USA
LVHW072341050221
678534LV00004B/37/J